At the Crossroads

At the Crossroads

*Not-for-Profit Leadership
Strategies for Executives
and Boards*

Philip Coltoff

WILEY

John Wiley & Sons, Inc.

Published by John Wiley & Sons, Inc., Hoboken, New Jersey.
Published simultaneously in Canada.

For general information on our other products and services or for technical support, please contact our Customer Care Department within the United States at (800) 762-2974, outside the United States at (317) 572-3993 or fax (317) 572-4002.

Wiley also publishes its books in a variety of electronic formats. Some content that appears in print may not be available in electronic books. For more information about Wiley products, visit our web site at www.wiley.com.

Library of Congress Cataloging-in-Publication Data:

Coltoff, Philip.
  At the crossroads : not-for-profit leadership strategies for executives and boards / Philip Coltoff.
       p. cm.
  Includes index.
  ISBN 978-0-470-61521-8 (cloth); ISBN 978-0-470-90664-4 (ebk);
  ISBN 978-0-470-90666-8 (ebk); ISBN 978-0-470-90667-5 (ebk)
  1. Nonprofit organizations–Management.   2. Leadership.   I. Title.
  HD62.6.C649   2010
  658.4′092–dc22   2010016369

Printed in the United States of America

10 9 8 7 6 5 4 3 2 1

To Lynn Harman, who served many roles in the course of the writing of this book—loving wife, severe but constructive critic, in-house editor, and professional ego-booster.

Contents

Foreword   xi
Preface   xv
Acknowledgments   xix

Introduction   **1**

Chapter 1   **Governance and Administration**   **7**
    Sarbanes-Oxley   8
    Accountability   9
    Organizational Culture   12
    Role of the Board   14
    Administrative Flexibility   17
    Summary   18

Chapter 2   **Roles and Responsibilities**   **21**
    Foundation Grants   22

	Government Grants	24
	Growing Your Fundraising	25
	Working with the Board and Staff	27
	The Social Safety Net	31
	Summary	32
Chapter 3	**Serving the Entire Community**	**35**
	How Location and Demography Affect Funding	36
	Broadening Your Service Base	37
	Serving the Community	43
	Summary	45
Chapter 4	**The Public Image of the Not-for-Profit**	**47**
	Making Your Not-for-Profit Visible	48
	Outcomes and Results	48
	Communication Strategy	50
	The Media and the CEO	51
	Branding	52
	Summary	54
Chapter 5	**The Social Work Professional—Manager and CEO**	**55**
	The Church, Immigration, and the Beginning of Social Services	56
	The Social Services Profession Evolves	60
	Managerial Roles in Social Services	65
	Summary	68
Chapter 6	**Programs and Priorities**	**71**
	Creating an Effective Mission Statement	72
	How Changes in Vision Affect Your Mission	73

Changing Direction   78
Summary   81

Chapter 7   **Public Policy and Government**
                Relations   **83**
                Bridging the Gap between
                  Independence and Advocacy   84
                Essential Steps to Being an Advocate   86
                Advocacy and Politics—Do They Mix?   87
                Summary   91

Chapter 8   **Lessons in Leadership**   **93**
                What Makes an Effective Leader?   93
                The Adaptive Leader   96
                What Makes Leaders Successful?   98
                The Role of the Manager   99
                Summary   100

Chapter 9   **The Board and the CEO**   **103**
                The Board of Directors   104
                The CEO   107
                Summary   110

Chapter 10 **Raising Money, Managing**
                Budgets, Building Relationships,
                and Thinking Ahead   **113**
                Not-for-Profits, Donors, and Funds   118
                Funds Management   120
                Summary   124

Chapter 11 **Evaluation, Human Resources,**
                Staff Training, and Development   **127**
                The Evaluation Process   128
                The Theory of Change   130

The CEO, Evaluation, and Human
    Resources   131
Responsibilities of the Human
    Resources Department   133
Staff Training and Development   136
Summary   137

Chapter 12   The Age of Technology   139
The Importance of Technology   140
Summary   143

Chapter 13   Volunteers and Voluntarism   145
The Growth of Voluntarism   146
Relationship between Volunteers
    and Management   147
Summary   151

**Chapter 14   International Social Welfare and
                the Role of the University   153**
Not-for-Profits' Increasing
    International Presence   154
Universities' Expanding Involvement   156
Summary   161

Chapter 15   Succession and Retirement   163
Who I Was and Who I Am Now   164
The Effects of Retirement on
    the CEO   165
Succession Planning   169
Summary   172

References   175
About the Author   179
Index   181

Foreword

This remarkable guide comes at a providential moment. Even as the American economy is groping slowly toward recovery, the great recession continues to exact painful costs, most of all for people in despair. For nonprofit service agencies, this is a time of triple trouble.

For one thing, the needs of the neediest have grown more acute. Hunger agencies say they are feeding 20 to 25 percent more people. Unemployment and underemployment afflict one of every six Americans. Millions of people, victimized by subprime deception and fraud, stand to lose their homes.

Meanwhile, the ability of nonprofit organizations to serve people in distress has declined sharply. At the New York Times Neediest Cases Fund, we experienced a drop of 5 percent in 2009 and a further drop of 9 percent in 2010, even though the number of donors was nearly flat. Other agencies report that their contributions are down as much as 25 percent.

These losses mirror the third source of trouble. Many nonprofits have relied on the annual income from endowments. Now, endowment gifts have become rare and existing endowments have shrunk drastically, chopping into the investment income that agencies have relied on to meet their operating expenses.

This turmoil and, on occasion, tragedy exposes a powerful need. All social services agencies, even those with experienced leaders, are driven to review and improve every operation, to sharpen every tool. This book, from the widely admired and longtime head of a famous agency, offers a series of wise lessons for all nonprofits, from new start-ups to established institutions.

Chapters 7 and 8 particularly warrant their close attention for they present two lessons that to me are misunderstood or poorly understood. One concerns advocacy. In Chapter 7, the author explains that yes, nonprofits are forbidden as a condition of retaining their tax-exempt status to support political candidates. At the same time, however, they are free to take public positions, even on the most controversial issues. Indeed, as he writes, they have a duty to take such positions, as "a logical extension of the organization's mission. The larger mistake is when an agency does not inform the community of the position that it is advocating."

Chapter 8 offers the second lesson, which, equally laudable, concerns the difference between management, as exacting and important as that is, and leadership. The key is vision and the author is at his best explaining why that's not just defining a dream but making it a driving force.

Phil Coltoff did that at the Children's Aid Society over four decades. In the words that follow, he turns that experience into a gift.

Jack Rosenthal, Senior Fellow,
The Atlantic Philanthropies, and former President,
The New York Times Company Foundation

Preface

Today's not-for-profit social services organizations face a challenging environment. Revenue sources are strained due to the economic recession and associated blows to state tax revenue and budgets. Compliance activities, including fiscal compliance, overdue attention to conflicts of financial interest, client confidentiality, and other regulations are required of today's not-for-profits, but seldom funded. The philanthropic public has been well tutored to equate low administrative overhead with quality in social services organizations. At the same time, the people who are served by not-for-profits are in great need, and are themselves negatively affected by the global recession and economic restructuring. Today's not-for-profits are expected to do more with less, and at the same time, to run like model businesses.

This is the challenging context that Phil Coltoff paints for today's not-for-profits.

In this book, Coltoff, one of the nation's most respected and longest-leading not-for-profit CEOs, shares the wisdom that he developed over decades as he led the nation's oldest children's services agency, the Children's Aid Society. Phil Coltoff's voice brings a balanced perspective, stressing leadership over technical challenges, and person-centeredness in the whole agency, from the board to the staff to the clients.

This book's contents provide a comprehensive analysis of the contemporary context and resulting challenges for not-for-profits. In addition to thoughtful reflections on the roles of the CEO in governance, board relationships, and roles and responsibilities including fiscal management, human resources, program development, and fundraising, Phil Coltoff pays careful attention to topics less frequently touched upon in not-for-profit management and leadership texts. He addresses the central role of public image and visibility of the not-for-profit to its multiple constituencies, including its funders, public and private, the community it serves, its clients, and its internal image. He reflects on the history of social services and the not-for-profit in America. He provides an insightful analysis of transformational leadership, including the central role of vision, strategy, and values. The latter part of the book addresses the cusp of tomorrow's challenges for not-for-profits, including leading in an era of technology, building the capacity for effective and responsible deployment of volunteers, the internationalization of social services in the context of globalization and shifting demographics, and finally, succession and retirement, one of the most critical organizational transitions for the CEO as well as for the organization.

Studies of social services show that we are about to enter an unprecedented phase of leadership transition with the retirement of the Baby Boom–generation CEOs. This book provides an outstanding resource to the aspiring generation of not-for-profit leaders. The wise master has spoken.

Lynn Videka, Professor and Dean,
Silver School of Social Work, New York University

Acknowledgments

Few books can be written without collaborators, many of whom play important roles and are often invisible. If writing a book were the equivalent of making a motion picture, the people whom I am referring to would be the stage manager, cinematographer, set decorator, costume designer, audiographer, musical director, and so forth. The music of a book requires this type of full ensemble to make it readable, let alone publishable.

In this spirit, I have many to thank. The first is the person to whom this book is dedicated, my wife, Lynn Harman. She truly was my in-house editor, spending hours on painstaking review, suggestions (sometimes made quite forcefully), editing, and proofreading. I can't imagine having been able to get through this work without her collaboration.

I thank the editors at John Wiley & Sons: Judy Howarth on copy and content and Susan McDermott on overall publication, cover, jacket, and everything else that falls in the category of publishing.

Thanks to my colleagues at New York University's Silver School of Social Work for their support—especially Dean Lynn Videka for her manuscript review and penning the Preface; and Jack Rosenthal, former President of the New York Times Company Foundation and Pulitzer Prize–winning journalist, for his encouragement and suggestions and for writing the Foreword. Michael Stoller, executive director of the New York Human Services Council, a colleague and friend, served as a peer reader.

Emerald Pellot, a student at NYU, who served as a work-study student assigned to me, was so helpful in many ways in getting my words on paper (or as it is these days, on the screen). I hope she also learned something from this process. A special nod goes to Bruss Del Valle and Alyssa Venere, who also pitched in, particularly with respect to the final edits. A thank-you goes to Lauren Moore, a colleague who reviewed the early manuscript. A special thank you also to Dr. Eileen Wolkstein, who reviewed the section on technology and made many helpful suggestions. And finally, thanks to the information technology staff at the Silver School of Social Work, ever-so-helpful and always available to me, Matt McGuirk and Andrew Harrison.

I am indebted and most grateful to all of these people for their wonderful assistance, support, and encouragement.

Introduction

The not-for-profit world is growing, changing, and becoming more complicated. The needs of consumers and the mandate to serve are rapidly increasing. As people age, they require health-related care from preventive services to end of life. Families are struggling to provide basic care for their children while many also have to care for their aging parents. Children's services are expanding from school or after-school programs to more complicated forms of institutionalization, community reentry, foster care, and help for the developmentally disabled.

Not-for-profits are found everywhere, from uncomplicated programs like Little League and community theater groups to very specialized centers for the treatment of mental illness and family disorganization. Not-for-profits dot our landscape from the community hospital to large

1

university-based medical centers, the Boys and Girls Clubs, settlement houses, senior citizen centers, food pantries, homeless shelters, school dropout vocational retraining programs, adolescent pregnancy prevention programs, and disaster-relief agencies. Not-for-profits, because of their size, budgets, and number of employees, are considered the third sector in American life, joining the for-profit free enterprise system and government. Not-for-profits are recognized as part of our social safety net, with government, through its umbrella of life-supporting services (such as Social Security, Medicare, food stamps, unemployment insurance, supplementary security insurance, Medicaid, and veterans' benefits), being the primary security blanket for most Americans, serving them from cradle to grave, healthy to sick, independent to dependent, and housed to homeless. The not-for-profit sector often fills the gaps and assures millions of Americans that the community stands ready to serve whether it is through assisted-living programs, preschool programs or after-school services for children, or meals on wheels for the hungry.

This third sector represents almost a million public charities with an even larger number of organizations that have been given tax-exemption status by federal and local government. It includes over 118,000 private foundations whose obligation it is to support the work of not-for-profit organizations such as educational, health, cultural, and social services. In 2007, public charities reported total revenues from all sources of over $1.4 trillion. Few nations in the Western industrial world have a gross national product that equals the not-for-profit revenues. This sector received $303 billion in private giving in 2009, with foundations contributing another $38.5 billion to support it in the same year (down 16.3 percent from 2008). The fact that our industry is so large and does so much does not mean that it is not in trouble. The recent deep recession has created huge gaps between the availability of resources and the needs of our citizens. In February 2010, unemployment was at 10.5 percent, the highest since the Great Depression. If those who have given up looking for work are factored in with underemployment, the figure is 17 percent of our total workforce. Over 25 million Americans without jobs require a variety of services in order to sustain themselves and their families.

During this period the number of homeless and food stamp recipients has risen to a level not seen since the 1930s, with demands on food pantries, homeless shelters, and employment services overwhelming many not-for-profit agencies.

Clearly, the job before us is huge. The need for services has increased exponentially for the poor, unemployed, homeless, idle youth, and runaway children. Family disorganization has increased, as has substance abuse, alcoholism, and child abuse, neglect, and abandonment. As the demands have increased, the supply has been put under enormous pressure. Not-for-profit budgets have been cut, government funding has decreased, contributions have fallen off by over 6 percent ($18 billion in 2008), and endowments and reserve funds have suffered the same proportional losses as has our stock market (between 20 and 30 percent). With this great loss of revenue, most not-for-profits had to reduce services, retrench staff, close facilities, and generally downsize operations.

The deep 2008–2009 recession caused us to look seriously at the crisis and effectively respond to people's needs. Even in better times, we need to reexamine our role, function, and place within society. Unfortunately, there will be other crises, future downturns in our economy, catastrophic occurrences, epidemics, and situations that we cannot predict. We need to be positioned so that we can respond quickly, effectively, and efficiently to any new situation. Along with government and private industry, not-for-profits' service providers must be ready to render assistance.

We must determine whether what we are providing matches the current needs. In this book, I examine how not-for-profits can address today's critical issues in ways that will help redefine their mission by expanding their vision. I examine the structure of not-for-profits, how they are governed, the role of the board of directors, and the responsibilities of CEOs. I explore the internal workings of not-for-profits in ways that can improve management, fundraising, public image, and capacity to reach and influence new donors. The reader will gain a better understanding of the relationship between not-for-profits and government. Funding, contracting, accountability, and partnering with governmental agencies are perplexing issues that are addressed. Leaders of not-for-profits, including the board, are faced with changing regulations, responsibilities, and liabilities. Times are changing and boards can no longer be complacent and uninvolved and simply attend monthly meetings. The board has a much larger role, as do the CEO and professional staff, in assuring fiscal and program accountability, service delivery, and sustainability of the agency. I examine these issues as well as branding, coalition building, lobbying, advocacy, and marketing.

The social work profession, which historically has been such an important part of the not-for-profit sector, also needs to look at its role and function during challenging times. I examine why fewer social workers are prepared and trained for leadership and top management positions in not-for-profits. The clinical role of social work, while important, has often eclipsed the training needed for social work's larger role in running the agencies where clinical practice takes place.

Universities are playing a greater role in preparing professionals for work in not-for-profits. Clinicians, practitioners, youth counselors, gerontologists, and employment specialists are being trained in colleges and universities. In addition, universities are the central location for social policy think tanks and institutes for social change. I explore how universities are becoming more global and need to play a significant role in assuring that our citizens receive a proper education that reflects our most pluralistic and democratic values.

I also examine the leadership qualities that executives need, why some not-for-profits succeed while others fail, and the characteristics of organizations that are on the way up as well those that are sliding into oblivion.

I identify the technologies required and the attention that must be paid to human resources, staff training and evaluation, and volunteers. I analyze the factors involved in leadership, retirement, and succession, noting that 60 percent of top leadership will retire over the next five to seven years.

The not-for-profit sector is a large, dynamic, instrumental, and absolutely essential safety net. *At the Crossroads* examines the issues that must be addressed for this industry to grow, meet its obligations, and secure its place in our country's social system.

Chapter 1

Governance and Administration

The structure of not-for-profits has always been of major relevance. Yet, officials of not-for-profits are often uninformed as to the history of the not-for-profit sector and even their own agencies. When was the agency founded? In what state was it chartered? What was its stated mission? Where are the articles of incorporation? Is there a written mission statement? These are some of the more significant issues pertaining to governance, but of course there is more information that both professionals and board members should know. What is the structure of the board of directors or trustees? How are board members selected? Is there a governance or nominating committee on the board? Does a code of conduct exist? Is there a conflict-of-interest statement? Is there a personnel practice manual? What are the legal and corporate history and mission of the organization?

All not-for-profits, especially those that enjoy a tax exemption [501(c)3], must have a governance structure starting with the existence of a board of directors, sometimes referred to as a board of trustees, board of governors, or board of overseers. The different terms grow out of the unique history of each organization and the relevant language that was used during the time of founding. All organizations require the existence of a legal body or board if they receive tax-exempt status or allow their donors to contribute to a legitimate charitable enterprise.

Sarbanes-Oxley

Many changes have occurred with respect to governance over the past five years. Some have been driven by federal and local oversight requirements and issues growing out of an enlarging philanthropic or charitable industry that has greater visibility and public scrutiny. At the federal level, the Sarbanes-Oxley (SOX) law, largely directed toward publicly held for-profit corporations, has had an enormous impact on the not-for-profit sector, even though it does not directly apply to or govern their operations. SOX raised the bar for oversight, transparency, and accountability. The application of SOX directed agency boards and individual members to seriously look at themselves and determine whether they possess the necessary knowledge, oversight, and system of review and accountability needed to effectively discharge their responsibilities.

The effect of SOX was so immediate that an entire industry of consultants quickly emerged to assist agencies in increasing their accountability mechanisms and responsibilities. Boards learned that they should establish an executive compensation committee, audit committee (to include independent participants), a nominating structure, and clear guidelines with respect to board conflict of interest and self-dealing. Board members of agencies took note and in both large and small not-for-profits a flurry of activity developed. Boards were both awakened and empowered to better understand their roles and responsibilities as directors. At the same time, these new requirements made some board members feel uncomfortable with respect to possible culpability. In some instances board members of not-for-profits had been asked by their employers to accept membership based upon the for-profit's interest in and significant grant to that agency. After SOX, many corporations and corporate foundations questioned whether they were assuming liability as a result of this practice. The corporate leaders did not want to expose themselves to or become culpable for the actions of the not-for-profit board, in which they had official representation. In many cases they withdrew their nominee and discontinued that practice. It is unclear at this stage whether the discontinuance had any significant impact on corporate grant making to not-for-profits. Many not-for-profits have found it more difficult to recruit directors, particularly from the corporate world, which has required agencies to find the funds to increase their directors' and officers' liability insurance policies.

Accountability

Even before SOX, the not-for-profit division of the Internal Revenue Service (IRS) offered both guidelines and directives with respect to some of the same issues raised in SOX. In some instances the IRS actually went further than SOX on proposing accountability measures. *Intermediate Sanctions,* an IRS ruling issued in the mid-1990s, prescribed penalties for agencies that did not have proper fiscal review, timely submission of reports, including 990s, which listed the compensation of their five highest-paid executives, and reporting of vendor and consultant compensation.

Intermediate Sanctions also raised questions about self-dealing of boards (vendor relationships) and defined acts of both commission and omission, which could result in penalties or even suspension of the organization's tax-exempt status. These new directives created a reexamination of roles, functions, and responsibilities of boards of trustees. The primary issue of transparency and accountability was heightened after alarming disclosures in the corporate world of Enron, World-Com, and giant banking enterprises. Not-for-profits, while not in the same league as these giant corporations, were nevertheless being held to a higher standard by government and within rating agencies in the private sector.

Clearly, not-for-profits and, of course, agency executive directors and CEOs should become thoroughly familiar with both SOX and all IRS, state, and local regulations that subject the agency and its board to review. The minutes of all board meetings as well as attendance of board members should be recorded accurately, and copies of the minutes should be stored carefully and sent to the agency's legal counsel for proper retention. Funding sources at the governmental level might request a review of the minutes, especially as it relates to their specific funding (e.g., Head Start, drug prevention or intervention, juvenile justice programs, mental health programs). Agencies might also consider having the minutes of their board meetings posted on the agency's website or in other ways made available to the public as a way of increasing notice and transparency.

At least annually, if not more often, attendance of board members at meetings should be reviewed by the nominating committee to determine whether members are sufficiently active to justify their continuation on the board. If board members do not attend at least 60 percent of all meetings, in person or through telecommunication, one should consider appropriate action. Some agencies have established advisory boards or councils that serve to keep board members interested and involved without legal responsibility. Council members are often invited to board meetings and events but are not voting members and do not have either responsibility or culpability for agency policy decisions.

Obviously all required reports should be submitted in a timely fashion, including all federal and local audits, program reports, and important collateral material such as conflict-of-interest statements, serious accidents or deaths that occur while a child is in custody of an agency, and Department of Labor submissions having to do with compliance with civil rights statutes. Where possible the board or one of its committees should be made aware of the content of these reports and in some instances actually participate in the discussions leading to their submission. Placing appropriate reports on an agency website can demonstrate to government regulators and the public that the organization is serious about transparency, public knowledge, and self-awareness.

In recent years, organizations such as the Better Business Bureau and CharityNavigator.com have established review guidelines for not-for-profit compliance and published their findings so that government, donors, and the general public have knowledge of the agency's fiscal and organizational adequacy. CharityNavigator.com applies a "star grading" system similar to a Zagat restaurant rating with respect to an agency's administrative and fundraising expenses relative to program expenditures—the lower the administrative expense, the higher the rating. While this practice is helpful, it can also cause agencies to unthinkingly reduce overhead costs to receive a good rating. Doing so can reduce the agency's capacity to supervise and monitor programs and assure quality control. While there is no single standard for administrative expenses relative to programmatic costs, all agencies should carefully review the ratio to assure funders that most of their donations or grants are going for service.

These days, most donors prefer not to give funds for management, supervision, and overhead. They usually designate a restricted gift for a specific program in which they have an interest and at times may instruct the agency not to use any of their gift for administration. This situation has caused many agencies enormous budgetary problems and has created a dilemma in supporting a program with inadequate funds for sound supervision or oversight. Agencies are especially grateful to donors who are wise enough to make grants for general operating expenses, knowing how essential those funds are to the sound operation of any organization.

Organizational Culture

Every institution has a culture that combines many elements, including mission, history, tradition, values, and rules and regulations. However, none of these elements is sufficient to define the culture—the overarching climate of the institution. It is both transmitted from generation to generation and reflective of the leadership of the board and the organization. The culture represents the heart and soul of the organization.

It has to do with issues of integrity, honesty, purpose, value systems, and fundamental respect for the client and confidentiality of that relationship. The culture, as I am defining it, drives and permeates the organizational behavior in ways that are more compelling than just a written code of conduct or rules and regulations.

While the culture may not be found in a specific paragraph in the agency's charter, it is a powerful force that creates a sense of the organization's importance and the expected behavior of those who are a part of it. We live in a world where competition, envy, and jealousy are often the rule rather than the exception. A culture that fosters teambuilding, respect, openness, and self-expression is counterpoint to that world. Often when professionals speak to one another about what makes a good agency as opposed to a marginal or bad one it is the culture that defines their judgment, not the official agency brochure, personnel practices manual, or website.

There are many examples of how the culture influences behavior. One involves a prominent CEO who was asked, "How can your organization govern the behavior of employees when the workplaces are far removed from the administrative hub and where oversight is difficult?" The CEO responded, "It's hard, but we do not compensate for this difficulty by installing a system of cameras or snoopervisors. What we have is a strong value system that speaks to what we believe in, what we stand for, and what our honor and merit system prescribes." Of course, the culture is not foolproof and cannot assure that wrongdoing or deviation do not occur, but when it is strong and infused with professional and humanistic values, it will be influenced positively. When the values of the culture become fully integrated, then it is akin to the honor system at a college or university. When the code or culture is violated, the entire team (employees) feels the weight of the wrongdoing and often imposes its own sanctions or recommends specific action to be taken. The informal system is at times the best barometer to measure how well the culture has been disseminated.

In specific terms, the culture of a not-for-profit should instruct employees that gossip in the workplace is not tolerated, breaking of confidentiality is not acceptable, and comments about a person's race, nationality, ethnicity, sexual orientation, or physical appearance will have no place in the institution.

The culture starts at the top and needs to be reinforced right through the agency's ranks at all levels. The culture needs to be lived, not just spoken of, and must be adhered to, administered, and enforced throughout the organization, not just left to the human resources department. The culture is sustained in staff meetings, agency newsletters and bulletins, the tone of the website, and the physical appearance of the workplace, where the atmosphere conveys a message of dignity and respect for all. The culture should never be taken for granted and must receive horizontal support throughout all departments of the organization, including the agency's board, CEO, and supervisory structure.

Role of the Board

In a later chapter I will discuss the makeup of the governing board, the relationship of the board to the chief executive, and the board's responsibilities (legal and policy) and their proper role and function. For purposes of this chapter, it is important to note that not only is the agency's very existence dependent on a well-functioning board, but the policies and direction of the board greatly affect and influence the culture of the organization. While the CEO is the primary administrator and contributes to and executes policy, the board often is the tone setter. As we know, professionals, including CEOs, are not permanent fixtures in an agency. They have mobility and often change between positions of leadership every five to eight years. The board, however, the one continuous and stable institutional mechanism, more often than not needs to be trained so that the agency's culture becomes incorporated.

In specific terms, the board, expressed through its leadership, must show respect for the agency's mission, staff, and work. This is especially the case when difficult work does not yield successful outcomes and despite best efforts does not achieve a positive result. When this occurs, the board needs to be supportive and maintain an atmosphere of understanding, not negative judgment.

Boards must recognize that much of the work of not-for-profits is akin to clinical trials and that results are often unpredictable. Try as we may, we do not yet have a formula for success. Failure in fact may be the best way for us to learn what does and doesn't work with respect to a particular problem. Whereas we strive for performance mastery and positive outcomes, we must recognize the limitations of our knowledge and practice skills. If the culture of the agency is to be sustained at a high level and if the agency is to be continually viewed in high regard, the board must play its role in adhering to and reinforcing the culture, which is central to a high level of professionalism.

As agency budgets have grown and become more difficult to sustain, and with fundraising efforts often falling short of their goals, many not-for-profits have considered establishing partnerships with other not-for-profits or merging with an agency of similar mission. Interestingly, this direction approximated the for-profit world where mergers and acquisitions almost became the order of the day. Fundraising organizations and clearinghouses such as The United Way encouraged organizations to share, partner, and in many cases merge as a way of reducing competition, saving money, and infusing new life into an existing organization. While some mergers make sense, boards and CEOs should look very carefully before leaping into something that may at a given moment seem attractive, particularly if a not-for-profit is struggling to meet its budget. Once a merger occurs, it is almost impossible to reverse course and the not-for-profit, its board, and its leadership will be subsumed under a different organization, culture, and style. What seemed compatible may indeed be incompatible and what appeared to be a shared vision may be more divergent than initially perceived. The best approach is to be cautious and not jump too quickly on the basis of immediacy unless it is in fact an opportunity to extend the service, reach more people, and help sustain the organization's life.

The board also has a fiduciary responsibility to carefully manage the agency's finances, particularly its reserve or endowment funds if they exist. Many older not-for-profits have accumulated endowment funds that were given by donors for specific purposes. The endowment income is often used for a designated program. Whereas the board has the legal responsibility for the management of the endowment, they also have the moral responsibility to use it in a prudent and responsible manner for the purposes stated. The relevancy of funds given years ago will no doubt need to be reassessed with respect to changes in our society and new needs that emerge. At times it is tricky to distinguish between restricted and undesignated endowment funds as determined by the donor, but it is nevertheless the responsibility of the board with the help of legal counsel to make ethical determinations with respect to the application of funds for new uses. Many universities and some community foundations have found themselves in difficult and touchy situations when they have arbitrarily applied endowment funds to programs or administrative costs without regard to the donor's original intention. The caution is again a real one; be careful, be ethical, and seek counsel.

Endowments should also be prudently managed. The not-for-profit board should carefully select investment managers who understand the nature and mission of the not-for-profit. The managers of the funds should not take undue risks and the board finance or investment committee should carefully monitor results. Investing the not-for-profit's endowment or reserve funds should not be viewed by either members of the board or the investment managers as being done in the same way as with their own personal investment portfolios. In recent years, too many endowments had a preponderance of funds in equities (stocks) rather than in a more balanced portfolio. When the market tumbled, so did their endowments, often causing the not-for-profit great budgetary hardship. If the funds had been prudently invested, the pain would have been less. Boards and fund managers should ignore the temptation to quickly make back that which was lost. The CEO should be knowledgeable about market fluctuations, should be a "governor" with respect to the use of reserves, and should help the board understand that the portfolio is an essential part of the agency's service capacity. Certainly the managers of not-for profit pension funds should invest more conservatively. These reminders are very important in helping the board take a more moderate and balanced position.

Administrative Flexibility

In recent years, many agencies have attempted to demonstrate flexibility with respect to employees by establishing

work-at-home child-care arrangements and special compensation for weekend or evening assignments. Many of these
arrangements are supportive of staff needs and demonstrate
a work atmosphere that encourages employee stability and
a high level of performance. Technology has allowed us to
make arrangements for employees to work at home. For those
whose jobs require field visits, traveling directly from their
homes saves precious time from having to report to the office
at either the beginning or the end of the workday. However,
there is one note of caution: Special arrangements should be
instituted in ways that are consistent, fair, and team building,
and that in no way overburden coworkers who do not enjoy these special flextime arrangements. Some not-for-profits,
believing that flexibility serves the agency well, have found
that it actually created a poorer workplace environment and
a competitive atmosphere where one did not exist before.

Summary

- Officials of not-for-profits, both staff and board, are often
  unaware of the organization's history, roots, and mission.
- Greater clarity needs to exist with respect to the structure
  of the organization's boards of trustees, selection process
  for board members, and the role of the nominating committee, in addition to a conflict-of-interest statement for
  board members and a code of conduct.
- Many new regulations governing charitable institutions
  similar to Sarbanes-Oxley, while not yet applicable to
  not-for-profits, need to be better understood.
- Board members have become increasingly concerned
  about their responsibilities, obligations, and culpability
  with respect to the organization.

- Various government agencies that fund programs run by not-for-profits periodically review agency minutes to determine whether the board is knowledgeable and informed about the program being funded.
- Board members should have performance reviews that include attendance at meetings, participation on board committees, and levels of contribution.
- Many not-for-profit organizations are now rated online by the Better Business Bureau and CharityNavigator.com. The ratings include administrative and overhead costs related to overall program budget.
- Not-for-profits should establish a "culture of work" that comes from the top and is reinforced on all levels throughout the organization.
- The human resources department, while responding to employee needs, is nevertheless an integral part of the organization's management structure.
- Failure is not to be feared, but understood as part of the learning process, much as are clinical trials in medical facilities.
- Boards and organizations should exercise caution before establishing mergers and partnerships to assure compatibility of mission and culture.
- The board and the executive should manage agency budgets and endowments prudently and with great care for future needs.

Chapter 2

Roles and Responsibilities

Not-for-profits have been caught in economic down-turns in ways that have caused much pain and great concern. During the past several years when the financial markets tanked, resulting in a general economic malaise, social agencies, commonly referred to as *not-for-profit organizations*, were squeezed between lesser resources and greater need. Why? Organizations that depended on private contributions were hurt because people tend to give less when they believe they are poorer or less able to share their wealth. Many wealthy donors or high-net-worth individuals, who often constitute the largest segment of a not-for-profit's donor base, immediately think reduction. In some instances these individuals, who often are still quite wealthy, but feel "poorer" because the market collapse resulted in a significant decline in their net worth, think first of their own needs and legacies and tend to be less generous and philanthropic. Others who constitute the contributing base and are not wealthy may also have no choice but to restrict their level of giving. During times of high levels of unemployment, some not-for-profit contributors have become recipients and in some instances requested services from the very organizations they had once assisted.

This sad state of affairs, largely based on economic realities, has resulted in across-the-board diminution of the contributing base throughout the country. Some not-for-profits have experienced as much as a 30 to 40 percent loss in contributions with others in the vicinity of 10 to 12 percent. The decrease in private contributions from individuals is often the first sign of an economic downturn. People understandably tend to hold onto their money longer, worry more about their own economic future, and think safety first, helping others last or not at all. Later in this chapter I look at ways to deal with this problem and suggest a number of approaches and remedies not merely to reduce this serious negative effect but to actually create a more conscious and educated public donor base that can serve the not-for-profit well during and after the immediate crisis.

Foundation Grants

While many not-for-profits rely heavily on private contributions, mostly from individuals, many organizations have also come to rely on foundation gifts. As we have realized with greater clarity during this period, most foundations invest their portfolios in the financial markets. Therefore it is not only businesses and individuals that have been hurt during the recession; foundations, universities, medical centers, and not-for-profit organizations also saw the value of their portfolios greatly decreased as the equity markets lost between 30 and 50 percent of their value.

Universities, even large and prestigious ones such as Harvard and Yale, have attempted to maximize their growth by investing parts of their portfolios in high-risk funds, derivatives, and private equity. The results from such ventures have ranged from poor to catastrophic. Foundations committed to supporting philanthropic efforts have experienced a considerable net loss in their portfolios that in turn resulted in a proportionate reduction in their philanthropic grants. Since the economic downturn beginning in 2007, a foundation that might have contributed $1 million to a large organization for a specific purpose might now reduce that gift by one-half or even one-third. The most notable and regrettable example is the Picower Foundation, which lost its entire corpus because of a suspect investment strategy, resulting in the immediate cessation of their gift giving. This was particularly hurtful since the Picower Foundation supported many worthwhile health, mental health, and community endeavors and was considered by agency executives as one of the most responsible and progressive foundations.

I will look into this issue in more detail to determine the approaches that agencies can employ in dealing with foundations and in diversification of their own fundraising, endowment management, and appeals.

Government Grants

When things get tight and the economy falters, government subsidies, contracts, grants, and at times even loans are usually the first to go down. We have certainly witnessed this during the last deep and serious recession. The student loan program for eligible college and university students fell below the line even before the news of excess profits derived by banks and accredited loan agencies became public.

Depending on the nature and mission of the social agencies, their budgetary dependence on government subsidy can vary from 0 to 100 percent. Many agencies whose mission is foster care and child care exist entirely on government reimbursement for their services. Youth-serving agencies such as settlement houses, Boys and Girls Clubs, Ys, and others of similar origin often depend on government contracts for between 40 and 80 percent of their operating budgets. The same can be said for those agencies whose primary mission is mental health and community development. In the community health area we know that the largest segment of their expenses will be reimbursed through Medicare, Medicaid, and other government funding streams such as Child Health Plus and Family Health Plus. Across the board, whether the not-for-profit is engaged in juvenile justice programs, food pantries, homeless shelters, preschool programs, Head Start, Home Start, or day care, government subsidy is the main or only source of revenue.

Often the client or consumer of these services is not even aware that the not-for-profit or private social agency servicing them is receiving government subsidies. Perhaps if more information were available to the public about government-sponsored programs voters might have a more positive attitude toward public financing in important areas such as health insurance, extended unemployment benefits, and services to veterans.

For the moment I am excluding the many underlying for-profits that in recent years have entered the social services provision field. These for-profits, particularly in the areas of home care for the elderly, home-based day care for children, and work internships for teens, tend to have a lower cost ratio even though they have a 3 to 5 percent profit built into their budgets. Many pay workers less than similar not-for-profit organizations and often exclude benefits. These for-profits of course are also affected by governmental cutbacks.

The not-for-profit, however, has a larger and longer-lasting mandate and needs to meet its costs without building in a profit margin. The main point is that very substantial elements of our social services network are largely dependent on government for its financial safety net. If the government cuts back, as it often does when budgets are tight, the negative fallout is enormous. Food pantries close, as they have in many instances, homeless shelters cease intake, Head Start programs shrink, and after-school programs dry up.

For good or ill, that is the existing relationship between social services agencies and government, which can determine whether individuals, families, and communities receive a needed service. Unfortunately, our sector does not enjoy the "too-big-to-fail" designation. We have no Federal Reserve Bank to come to our aid. Perhaps we should, but that's just not the present reality.

Growing Your Fundraising

Let's look at what not-for-profits can do to improve their fundraising capacity during times of stress. The first is not to lament one's fate, say the situation is terrible, receive some solace that others are in the same position, and decide to do nothing while hoping that things will improve as the economy gets better. Agencies need to sustain their services *now* and clients cannot and should not have to wait for things to improve. Here are some tips that may be helpful:

- Be brave—inform your donors that your situation is bleak, that you are down x percent in your fundraising, and that you need help desperately. Share your concerns and let them know what essential services you may have to reduce or cut if people like them do not respond.

- Increase your visibility—make your case to the public by reaching out to the media for free Public Service Announcements (PSAs) and invite newspaper and broadcast media coverage of your programs and, once again, let the public, through the media, know of your grave situation. Make your case strongly and where possible and appropriate use consumers or clients to tell the story. They often do a better job than you can.

- Search for a donor or group of donors who recognize the situation and are ready to step forward. Have them sign customized letters to others in your donor base asking them to continue or enlarge their gifts during these hard times. The donor's message should be, "I'm ready to give more. Are you?"

- Arrange low-cost house parties where the host provides simple refreshments and the guests include potential donors. Make it local, brief, and to the point. If the host lives in a particularly nice area or has an especially lavish home or apartment that people want to see, even better. Ask for contributions right then and there after a brief presentation.

- Reach out to funders you have researched and believe are interested in your not-for-profit, offering them an opportunity for "ownership" in a particular service. People want to feel their contribution is going to a designated program that is important to them.

- Finally, do not assume that a one-time gift will not be sustained for three or more years. Adult children of the donor as well as other family members might also be interested in your work. Invite members of the family to visit your agency and see the program or site that needs their help. Take them away from a corporate-looking office and into your field of work. It makes a difference.

Working with the Board and Staff

Your board or governing body also has a particular role that should not be overlooked during this period. First, keep your board totally informed, hide nothing, be transparent, and have the board understand that this is not your burden alone but theirs to share. The board should understand that at times "Keynesian economics" (spend more during bad times and replace those funds when times improve) works in social agencies, too. At the same time, you do not want to panic the board and have them make decisions in a crisis atmosphere which are not sustainable. If the agency has a reserve fund or endowment, invading it should be done with care and the principle of replacement should always be kept in the forefront. The board should know that careful management of the present situation is most important and that you are not contemplating growth without the resources to manage and sustain those new services. The board will be relieved if they know that you are on top of the situation and your recommendations are clear, thoughtful, and well-developed. There is no need to panic and sell off agency assets like buildings and at the same time no need to randomly slash services across the board. If selective cuts have to be made, they should be done carefully and with full participation of relevant staff and board. Obviously, board members, where possible, should increase their own gift-giving during this period to reflect the need for additional resources by setting an example and hopefully a trend for others.

Before I leave this important discussion on the role of the governing board, I must note that the executive should engage the board on a continuing basis in a discussion relative to agency growth, strategic planning, and a review of services that will be continued or discontinued within a specific timeline. An exit strategy should also be part of the planning process and key members of your staff should be aware of it. Such planning should not only occur during times of crisis but should be a part of the ongoing work of the agency and of its operation, including the Board of Trustees (strategic and long-range planning).

During hard times while government cutbacks are prevalent, new opportunity often comes to the surface. The executive and his or her team should be aware of new opportunities to work with government and secure governmental subsidies. This may seem contradictory, but let's look at what is happening today. The stimulus package substantially increased dollars for preschool services, Head Start, health-related services, after-school educational academic services, programs for the unemployed, and child abuse and neglect prevention. These programs are receiving great attention and have been earmarked for funding. What this means is that agency executives and their boards primarily need to be aware of what is happening in the marketplace at various levels of government.

Agencies should belong to coalitions and partnerships that can provide this information since most do not have a public policy staff; they should be ready to see whether their agency's mission fits the new direction and/or whether their vision presents an opportunity for mission expansion to capitalize on these new funding streams. I am not suggesting "chasing the dollar," but rather flexibility and elasticity in reviewing service priorities and establishing a comfort zone in shifting agency agendas based on need and situation.

Key agency personnel including the executive director (ED) should take the lead with respect to finding new sources of revenue. Often this is left to the development department or the fundraiser. Those folks can help, but when it comes to outreach to either private givers or governmental authorities they want to see the top man or woman. I can't stress this enough: The executive director cannot delegate this task. Once it is determined where the sources of revenue are (for example, in the stimulus package), you should go to the source, be it Washington, D.C.; the state capital; or City Hall. You should not wait for the request for proposals (RFP) or the public comment to become proactive. Often that's too late. You should be aggressive, find out who the right people are in which governmental agency, and find appropriate ways of knocking on their door. If you are to be ahead of the curve, then you have to take these steps very seriously and understand that waiting for the information is the equivalent of standing at the back of the line. Those who are aggressive get to the right people, understand the right sources, and most importantly begin the process of relationship building that is the key to capturing the prize. There are only so many prizes to capture, and those who are on the wait list are not going to get seated. I cannot emphasize this enough. This topic deserves greater explanation, which you will find in

Chapter 1, on governance, and Chapter 3, on serving the entire community.

Much of what I have discussed is true not only about government but also in the foundation world. Foundation leaders have said that while clarity of purpose, mission, and past performance are relevant, relationship and personal trust trumps all other considerations. This being the case, the trust that is established between the agency executive and the director of development is central to securing foundation gifts. Here are some more tips:

- Clarity and brevity in a proposal response is important; nobody wants to read a 20-page proposal if 2 pages would do. Length is not a barometer of clarity.
- Research and evaluation are valued very highly today and used to confirm and support the work and interventions on any particular topic or issue. If evaluation results are available on a given topic, they should become central to the proposal. In some instances even short-term evaluation, questionnaires, and self-reports will help on the submission of an application to a foundation. Don't be bashful; use the tools at your disposal.
- Evidence-based interventions are given a strong measure of support. While new and experimental work may not yet have evidence to support its efficacy, much of our work can be supported by evidence assembled either by us or other organizations. Evidence-based programs, also referred to as *outcome funding*, should help us in our submissions to foundations.
- Know what the foundation executive is interested in. Listen, try to arrange a pre-interview before a written submission, and don't assume that what you're submitting is necessarily congruent with the foundation's direction

or interest. Many foundations today are not interested in merely giving money and then getting a report a year later. They want to be part of the process, the review, and the midcourse corrections as well as the outcomes. It is in your best interest to connect to the foundation executive, build a relationship, and not view the funder as an outsider or intruder. This does not mean that you give up your mission, autonomy, or responsibility. Engagement is an important principle.

- Be ready to form partnerships with other agencies that are dealing with similar issues. Your proposal should speak to this issue and if operational partnerships are not appropriate, then you should look at how to communicate and disseminate information to other agencies and the field.
- Finally, use technology. Every program should be on the agency's website or in some instances a separate website if the program is very large. Communication through this medium is most important; without it most programs suffer both lack of visibility and opportunity.

The Social Safety Net

In the recently published book *This Time Is Different: Eight Centuries of Financial Follies* (Princeton University Press, 2009), by Carmen M. Reinhart and Kenneth S. Rogoff, the authors state that "policy-makers and business leaders step forward and say that nobody should be fearful ... bubbles have burst before...." While this quote reflects a belief that we will come out of the deep recession intact, with our financial institutions surviving and investors recovering from their unrealized losses, it disregards the unremitting harm done to millions of people .

with respect to loss of jobs and medical coverage and a sense of hopelessness for their future.

The not-for-profit world remains the essential safety net and provides for those least able to provide for themselves. Beyond public assistance, food stamps, housing allowances, and childcare provisions, we offer a renewed sense that they matter, they are not invisible, and our social system cares about their well-being.

Eric Zencey, professor of political studies at Empire State College, stated in a recent article in the *New York Times,* "Let's stop focusing on just economic activity, and let's start tracking well-being. Our job is the restoration or protection of the quality of life."

Boards and executives of not-for-profit institutions should reassess their mission and service priorities. Counseling, recreation, child care, and mental health services must find new approaches to serving those in need. Everything involved in helping eligible families enroll for health insurance, child care, food stamps, Supplementary Security Income, and other forms of financial assistance should become part of the not-for-profit's ongoing service package. After all, this is what our country and our clients need at present and in the future.

Summary

- In difficult economic times some donors may actually become recipients of services and need assistance.
- Managing the drop-off in contributions and reduction in donor base is an ongoing responsibility.
- Faulty endowment or investment strategies by charitable agencies and foundations often contribute to the crisis.

- Government funding reduction affects not-for-profit services and delivery systems.
- Not-for-profits need to improve their fundraising capacity and posture, increase visibility, seek new donor bases, expand outreach, request donors to do more, and secure greater trustee giving and support.
- Board understanding of the financial crisis and the needs of clients must be secured during difficult times. The board may need to use additional reserve or endowment funds or rainy-day set-asides, or engage in responsible borrowing to meet the crisis.
- Board and executive staff should engage together in the process of service reductions, budget cutting, and staff downsizing. Responsibilities should be shared between board and staff for these decisions.
- The crisis can help create new opportunity. Agencies should reassess their mission and service delivery in light of the present need.
- The executive director should lead the process of change and be the key person to connect to both governmental agencies and potential new funding sources. The ED should be the key face of the agency.
- Proposals to funding sources should be clear and brief, reference evaluation, and be evidence based where possible. Partnerships should be explored with respect to both foundations and other not-for-profits.
- The continuous need for not-for-profits to reassess their mission should be unrelated to crisis management.

Chapter 3

Serving the Entire Community

Not-for-profits can be viewed in three different spheres of service. The first is comprised of those larger agencies that serve a broad sector of the community. They can be national or local, but even when national their affiliate branches serve local jurisdictions (e.g., the Boys and Girls Clubs of America, Big Brothers Big Sisters, the Red Cross, 4H Clubs, and Girls Inc.). The second sphere is made up of those that are specifically local and have charters that call for them to serve a specific state or jurisdiction within a state. They may have broad scope to provide many services and in some instances may have interstate compacts for purposes related to adoption and foster care, among others. The third sphere is characterized by local agencies defined by a specific geographic area or demographic. Most agencies fit into this last category—for instance, a settlement house that serves the Woodlawn section of Chicago, Illinois, or a community school in the Allston/Brighton section of Boston, Massachusetts. The larger the city and the more diverse the population, the greater the likelihood that not-for-profits will serve specific, clearly defined populations and communities.

How Location and Demography Affect Funding

In New York City and other large cities, funding sources may offer agency contracts or grants for a specific service in a specific location, such as foster care preventive services in a distinct community, which then delineates the population within. Government funds might be denied to that agency if it served people outside of the community district without receiving a waiver or prior permission. In a large city where 80 or 100 agencies provide similar services (foster care prevention), reducing duplication and competition while still providing options is very important. It also becomes clear to the residents or clients of that community which agency is better able to serve them and has the obligation to provide a specific service dimension (for instance, after-school and preschool programs or foster care prevention or reentry of juvenile offenders).

Other local agencies may not have a defined geographic area but rather a very well-defined service population. A Boys and Girls Club might serve only youngsters ages 6 to 18 who live in a geographically defined community. A settlement house, however, may have a broader mandate serving children, teens, young adults, and senior citizens. Some not-for-profits define their services on the basis of mission and not geography or demographics. The mission of a not-for-profit becomes the major determinant for what is delivered to a specific community, an entire borough, or the city at large, such as serving those who are temporarily homeless, have a substance abuse issue, are unemployed and need job training, or are high school dropouts.

The spectrum of voluntary not-for-profits cuts across many areas of urban or rural life. Some years ago, not-for-profits described their services in even more specific ways. Some indicated that their services were geared only to those of a specific gender, nationality, or ethnic background. Some used an economic yardstick to determine who would receive their services. Today, some not-for-profits with some justification still describe what they do in very clear terms: Girls Inc. makes no apology for directing its services to girls from latency to young adulthood. Some agencies might refer to their mission as serving African American boys who have been incarcerated and their programs might relate to either legal representation or their return to the community. Still others would define their purpose as working with status offenders—youngsters who because of their age have not committed a crime but are nevertheless court referred for truancy, incorrigibility, or being ungovernable.

Broadening Your Service Base

Today most agencies have a broader mandate. Some years ago, the Boys Clubs of America wisely chose to become the

Boys and Girls Clubs of America, eliminating any possibility of gender discrimination or sexism within their organization, and by doing so expanded their mission. Such is the case for many organizations that desire to be less sectarian and more pluralistic. This was and is the case for organizations that grew out of a faith-based orientation—Catholic Charities, Jewish Community Centers, and YMCAs. These organizations still have their religious or ethnic group as the primary recipient of their programs, but they have broadened their base to include those outside of their religious or cultural group. Today, most Catholic parochial schools in New York City have enrolled more non-Catholics than Catholics. Jewish, Protestant, and Catholic-sponsored agencies that serve foster children, as well as those that deliver mental health or juvenile justice programs, do not limit their outreach and deliver exclusively to their own religious group. It would be difficult to secure government funds for those services if they chose to limit eligibility to those of their faith. Quite aside from legal precedent our philosophy and direction has changed.

Most agencies no longer institute a "means test" to determine eligibility. There is a general understanding that people who need service or assistance should not have to produce income tax returns or rent receipts before help is provided. However, some government programs such as food stamps and rent subsidies require a means test. In most instances, help should not be limited to those in need who fall under or over a predetermined income line. Though society still views social services as a privilege, not a right, we are nevertheless moving in the direction of a more open and less restrictive set of rules for eligibility.

While the Puritan ethic reinforces the idea that people should take care of their own and come to the "community" for help only when they are desperate, in crisis, or in an emergency, the prevailing view is no longer wedded to that concept. We know that a person can be fully employed, have health insurance, take care of his or her children, be a responsible citizen, and in a flash lose his or her job, benefits, and sense of security. When this happens, the crisis is not an individual problem or weakness but rather a problem embedded in our social system. Millions of people whose jobs were lost in 2009 have struggled to find work. With the health insurance reform bill, now law, more than one half of the 50 million Americans currently without health insurance can now be insured. Nevertheless, millions of children, immigrants, and undocumented people will be left outside the health care system. Unemployment is endemic; 30 percent of high school students did not graduate in 2009 and more than one half of teenagers who are looking for jobs cannot find one. These big issues created a shift in social services and helped change the public attitude of what constitutes an individual crisis or failure versus a dysfunction within our social system.

The *New York Times* reported on October 22, 2009, that New York City residents receiving food stamps reached 1.6 million in August 2009, a surge of nearly 30 percent in two years. This unprecedented increase in eligibility for food stamps reflected the recession and the numbers of unemployed. Are social agencies stepping up to the plate to help secure this needed service for their client group? Too often agencies continue on a narrow path providing only one service disconnected from other essential services that *their* clients need. A change in our modus operandi is obviously called for. Similarly, Nicholas D. Kristof wrote in his August 19, 2009, *New York Times* column how inexpensive it would be to provide health care coverage to those who are eligible as compared to the costs of incarcerating someone who might steal a pair of socks worth $2.50. It is silly, he suggested, to deny people a service or an entitlement, have them commit a nonviolent crime, and then have the taxpayer commit a fortune in incarceration costs. In California, that cost is estimated at $216,000 annually for each inmate compared with only $8,000 for each child attending the troubled Oakland public school system. The cost to keep children in school until 6:00 P.M. through an academically enriched after-school program in some cases can add as little as $1,000 per child for a modest two-hour program. More comprehensive programs including parent outreach, compensatory educational enrichment, and summer camps can double or triple the costs. All of these programs keep children safe and out of harm's way during the high-crime hours of 3:00 P.M. to 7:00 P.M.

The Trust for America's Health, an organization affiliated with The Centers for Disease Control, informed us that two-thirds of Americans are now overweight or obese, and that percentage is rising. The study defines *overweight* as a body mass index (BMI) of 25 to 30 and *obesity* as a BMI of over 30. It points out that racial and ethnic factors may affect this measurement and therefore the risk is greatest for non-Europeans. While we have become painfully aware of these statistics, one wonders how many human services agencies have reached into their toolkits to establish programs that address the issue of obesity. How many have enriched their nutrition and dietary programs, added physical health to their after-school or recreation programs, and established individual and team sports activities on weekends? If we begin to see our role and mission as being more integrated and coping with present needs, we can address these issues in a much more fundamental and comprehensive way. Obviously, we still need government assistance. With the 2009 stimulus and education bill, coupled with the summer jobs employment programs, such assistance is available but the responsibility falls on us to organize the programs, hire appropriate staff, and show that what we are doing makes a difference. Many new funding sources, some directly through the U.S. Department of Education, Health and Human Services and the Department of Justice, are there to be tapped by resourceful nonprofits. I hope and trust that we are ready for these tasks.

The events of September 11, 2001 helped change attitudes toward those who were primary or secondary victims who lost their jobs and homes. People of all persuasions, economic backgrounds, races, and nationalities came to community agencies seeking help. The Red Cross and Federal Emergency Management Agency (FEMA) were the primary disaster-relief agencies, but every community-based program found people waiting at its doors suffering from a variety of ills, needing relief, counseling, and assistance. Agencies across the board, whether they were settlement houses, YMCAs, schools, churches, or government programs, rose to the occasion and seldom turned clients away. They may have referred clients to the Red Cross for housing or food supplements, but most agencies used their professional staffs to provide a variety of other services during this time of crisis. The events of 9/11 changed the orientation and metric of service.

Categorical funding from government often prevents an agency from expanding its services to clients in programs such as Head Start, foster care, or senior centers. The nature of the funding might prohibit the provider from reaching out to family members who need the service but are not defined as the primary recipient. While such government contracts are commonplace, many not-for-profits have objected to this type of funding because it is so rigidly applied, and limits staff capacity to broaden their service outlook and provide a more comprehensive service. An example of this would be a family who enrolls their child in a Head Start program but cannot receive assistance under this "categorical funding" to serve a slightly older brother or sister in an after-school program. One can easily see how disjointed this approach can be in limiting the opportunity to provide an integrated service to fix a problem and serve a family.

A better system can be developed to ensure that people in need receive help without limiting a provider's opportunity. Advocates are not necessarily suggesting that all government dollars be fungible but rather flexible in application. A system of accountability and fiscal and program audits should be built into the process to insure that the designated funds are not improperly used. In this discussion I am excluding the application of a means test to determine eligibility for public assistance, food stamps, housing subsidies, and disability relief. Those requirements established by Congress are usually implemented by governmental agencies and do not present a problem for not-for-profit providers. Clearly, advocacy organizations and others devoted to an examination of the social system have a role to play in helping our policymakers provide greater access to those in need.

Our social agency network is considerably more comprehensive than in the past and so large that it is often referred to as the third sector with private industry and government being the first two. The total expenditure in our sector if viewed in gross national product (GNP) terms would make it the seventh or eighth leading country in the world.

With the many positive changes recently made there are still gaps and holes in the system that discourage a broader and more complete social services network. Clients are often bumped from agency to agency with the words, "Unfortunately, we do not provide that service, but the agency down the block does." While information and referral are very important elements, a single not-for-profit agency cannot provide everything that a client needs. We know that information and referral alone are not the answer. The notion that a client who really wants and needs help will be motivated and mobile enough to get to the proper source is antiquated and erroneous. Clients referred to other agencies often do not get to their destination unless there is follow-up, a transportation allowance, or an escort service.

"One-stop shopping" is becoming more available in large service systems such as community schools, settlement houses, and centers that offer a variety of services, including government programs such as food-stamp eligibility and distribution, built right into the social services center. These larger, community-friendly centers have established considerable trust with neighborhood residents and provide a whole system of services that do not require sending someone to another source, thus fragmenting the family. Some one-stop programs include pre-school services, after-school services, teen groups, parent drop-in resource rooms, recreational and weekend services, and some government programs. Confidentiality of service is of course maintained when counseling and mental health programs are a part of the one-stop mix. One program that deserves mention is Single Stop, particularly now that it has gone national.

Serving the Community

There are also broader issues with respect to serving a community. We often speak of the not-for-profit as providing not only a safety net but a vehicle for the promotion of sound citizenship. The not-for-profits are in a unique position not only to serve people in need, but also to connect them to their environment. This approach toward multiculturalism is as sound today as it was years ago when social agencies became the mechanism for introducing immigrants to our country.

We know that while social agencies themselves do not have the power to change housing patterns or school districts, they can and in some instances have broadened their base to unite people of different backgrounds. Community centers, settlement houses, and YWCAs are in the best position to use their facilities, summer camps, day camps, and teenage outreach programs to bring people together and provide programs that allow for a discussion of differences and stereotypes. This work is among the most important we do since it raises the bar from the provision of a specific helpful service to a larger role of education and acculturation and helps to preserve our democracy. We must recognize that over the next 20 years the majority of the U.S. population will be made up of relative newcomers: Latinos, Asians, West Africans, and those from the Caribbean, combined with African Americans, who presently make up 13 percent of our population. Social agencies have a powerful role to play within this heterogeneous environment, unlike any that we have had since the late nineteenth and early twentieth centuries.

To accomplish this important strategic mission we must carefully look at our programs to determine the relevance and the composition of our staff and boards. The makeup and configuration of our agencies have been ignored for too long. Our board executives and staff should not only reflect the ethnic, racial, and national makeup of our cities but also anticipate what our cities will look like in the future. This requires an agency to look at itself carefully, complete a self-study or inventory, and review its governance, board nominations, and hiring procedures. As discussed in Chapter 1, "Governance and Administration," we must recognize that the image projected to a community is important.

We must also move beyond social class. The poor, needy, dispossessed, and disenfranchised need and deserve our attention, but we should not overlook those in the traditional working class who have lost their health insurance, are struggling to keep their jobs and families intact, and are part of the broader community. Some years ago, a number of colleagues coined the phrase "Serving the poor exclusively often becomes a poor service," meaning that unless we understand (and receive support from) the full community we risk it turning against us and not providing the sanction we need to exist.

Unfortunately, many of our social agency leaders unintentionally alienate large groups of the community who support our work—the voters, contributors, and during tough times, recipients. We must resist the temptation to think narrowly and understand that in the long run it is the broader community that will determine the support we receive and in some instances the existence of our agencies.

Summary

- Some not-for-profits are national or international in nature while others serve a specific geographic community or demographic group.
- Funding is often for a specific service, in a specific community, serving a well-defined population. At times the funding is so specific that it is neither flexible nor fungible.
- Not-for-profits often have redefined their mission to have a broader mandate and be less limited in scope.
- Most agencies who serve the poor no longer institute a means test to determine eligibility for the service.
- Social agencies have an obligation to change their modus operandi so as to allow them to serve clients in a more responsive way.

- Recent events, including 9/11, earthquakes, tsunamis, and other disasters, have caused not-for-profits to broaden their service outlook.
- Advocates are now stressing the flexible use of governmental dollars in ways that remain accountable but not categorically limited.
- The not-for-profit sector, the third sector after private enterprise and government, is growing and has considerable influence.
- Agency executives, boards, and staffs should reflect the ethnic, racial, and national makeup of population.

Chapter 4

The Public Image of the Not-for-Profit

This is the power of the flywheel. Success breeds support and commitment, which breeds even greater success, which breeds more support and commitment—round and around the flywheel goes. People like to support winners!" This quote from *Good to Great and the Social Sectors* (HarperCollins, 2005), by Jim Collins, speaks to the need to gain public support or "community sanction." Collins describes what is involved in building a great institution. While acknowledging that there is no one silver bullet or "killer innovation," there are ways to push the flywheel forward—inch by inch, until it completes an entire turn. He writes, "You don't stop pushing, and if you do it in a consistent and intelligent way the flywheel moves a bit faster." Collins writes about the need to advance the work of the not-for-profit in ways that gain the attention and recognition of the larger community of policymakers, the media, the political establishment, and the public at large. This takes us to the issue of public image, marketing, and branding.

Making Your Not-for-Profit Visible

All institutions, including not-for-profits, need to have a public face, and one that is recognizable. The mission and work of the not-for-profit need visibility whether the public face is directed to a funding or policy source or internal or external relations. Not-for-profits that do wonderful work—and in some instances indispensable work—are often the best kept secrets in town. They tend to have limited budgets and most executives in these agencies direct most of their available funds to service activities, leaving little budgetary room for administration and even less for public relations, research and development (R&D), and outreach. This is understandable but a big mistake. Our industry, to grow and survive, needs *public and community sanction*. People must know why we exist, what we do, why we do it, what we achieve, and why they should support us. If we do not find ways and use available vehicles to achieve this objective, then we pigeonhole ourselves and create a closed and invisible environment. It is not boastful to let people know what we are doing and how well we do it.

Outcomes and Results

We must go beyond the traditional means of in-house newsletters, donor and prospect mailings, and annual reports.

These days, technology is king and agencies that do not have active and updated websites will be left behind. Even dollar contributions now come in online, let alone information about the work of the organization. An effective website is the best way for an organization to be both transparent and visible to many publics.

Funders especially want results, often referred to as *outcomes* or *deliverables*. Organizations that can direct some of their resources toward evaluation of their programs are ahead of the game and can honestly state, "This is what we've achieved: We've reduced the number of domestic violence cases by 20 percent; our random sample shows that fewer young girls attending our programs become pregnant; 60 percent of the children in our Head Start program do better when entering first grade than those who are not in the program. . . ." Get the message? Stating and justifying evaluation outcomes using scientific means where possible and acceptable metrics make the case. Evaluation does not have to be complicated. Where possible, doing random selection with a control group is best, but other, simpler forms of outcome evaluation are also important and should not be underestimated. Questionnaires to parents and teens, self-reports, attendance data, and reductions in arrest rates for youngsters in programs are all reportable data. As long as we are honest and can back up our findings we should promote what we do.

There are many other ways to reach the public that unfortunately many not-for-profits are not aware of or do not utilize. Regular or monthly roundtable breakfasts or inviting present or potential donors works well, as do press briefings, outreach to selective audiences such as trust officers of banks to encourage bequests, and active communication with people in the media. Many executives of not-for-profits are fearful of media attention and avoid it. Some of this is due to the media looking for negative press about the not-for-profit, such as an overlooked abused child, a drowning in a supervised swimming pool, or a poorly assessed home visit. The media does tend to focus on bad news, but that doesn't always have to be the case. If we connect to people in the media who trust us, they will learn about the good things we do and the help that we provide, such as the reduction of gang violence, or the avoidance of a crisis. Given the opportunity, more often than not they will respond positively.

Communication Strategy

Every organization should have a communication strategy that is integrated into the organization's overall strategic plan. Communication is a large topic and includes media, marketing, and public relations with a host of constituencies. Most of what managers do every day is communicate with staff, board members, volunteers, donors, government, agencies, the public, and the media. A simple exercise for creating a media strategy is to list the key tasks assigned to each member of the organization and then have them think about the news value of their work. What is the organization doing that might make a good news story? How can getting that story into the media help you? Consider everything the organization does from the perspective of the media and the possible advantages and disadvantages of getting coverage of a particular program, action, or policy. Writing news releases does not have to be complicated; keep it simple, assume nothing, determine your audience and why the release is worth writing, and connect the dots (issues, causes, etc.).

The Media and the CEO

Agency executives need to be in the forefront of this outreach. Yes, we can get help from people in the public relations world, but the face of your work needs to be your face; you need to speak for the agency. Think about it: Would you trust a subordinate, however intelligent, to speak for the president, when it is the president you want to hear from on a major issue? You as chief executive must be comfortable in the arena of public relations and marketing. You need to be clear, on message, knowledgeable, and ready and comfortable in taking credit when it is due or blame if things do not go right. When the chief executive gains this level of recognition over a period of time, those in the media will reach out to him or her when issues related to that organization's work come to the forefront. The media people will call you for comment on public issues, proposed legislation, and controversial subjects. They may want you to be critical of the way government or another agency has handled a particular issue, but once they learn that you are available, forthright, open, and honest, your voice will be heard. Agency leaders should also write editorial comments or letters to the editor and op-ed pieces. You may have to write ten op-ed pieces before one will be published but that depends on the newspaper, its size, and its circulation. Outreach is important and describes your agency's position and differentiates it from other organizations.

The media, especially print, does not like bland, righteous, or polemical articles. They do like controversy and very often will respond to an article that is appropriately critical, takes a stand, and is in opposition to existing policy. Executives should recognize this but also know that facts gained through knowledge, evaluation, and results are what justify the position that the agency is taking. You need to be comfortable in backing up what you say or write and have the information and facts at your disposal.

Branding

John Gardner, former secretary of Health, Education and Welfare and the founder of Common Cause, once said, "No organization's brochure should be better than the program that it describes." That is a truism all organizational leaders should heed. We should not overstate what we do or try to enhance our image in ways that are merely promotional. Too many not-for-profits, in an attempt to secure funding or recognition, exaggerate and over-claim what they do and are then embarrassed when called on it. Most organizations have plenty of good things to announce and advertise without having to reach into the stratosphere. Keep this in mind.

Branding has always been important but has become even more relevant today. How do we differentiate ourselves from others? How do people know our product? How do we effectively tell our storyline? All of these issues go into branding. Organizations should regularly review their annual reports, and their logo, including the color associated with the organization and its tagline. JPMorgan Chase, for example, is identified with the color royal blue. Once you see that color and logo you know it is Chase. Color is part of branding and so is a tagline. The Boys and Girls Clubs of America use "A positive place for kids." It is everywhere and has been picked up by the media. Major League Baseball and the United Way all refer to the Boys and Girls Clubs of America with that particular tagline. It is what people remember. The tagline and color should also be on the website, annual report, newsletters, and where possible, the program folders and brochures. Banners, tablecloths, and merchandise should also display the same logo, color, and tagline whenever the organization is sponsoring an event or dinner. These are all important ways to identify the organization uniquely in the public's mind and to distinguish it from other organizations.

Branding and marketing should also work in parallel with strategies developed for private giving. Building and reinforcing the brand requires continuous and consistent attention. Organizations can find their own appropriate tagline that in a single sentence describes the function of the organization, such as "We fill the gap," "We keep kids safe," and "We are the fun place to be." You get the message. Branding and marketing do not have to be expensive. Securing sponsorship for events is important and when that occurs the sponsor and not-for-profit's market strategies should be employed.

The extent to which not-for-profit organizations are at the forefront of public issues and events will provide the visibility needed to affect positive change and place organizations at the cutting edge. David Brooks, in the August 27, 2009, *New York Times*, was spot-on when he indicated that leadership skills have matured in ways that combine clear statements of principle with pragmatic approaches. He suggested that speaking to principle must also be accompanied by a practical, incremental approach. We should raise our voices on important social and political matters of the day but always understand that we must be strategic and propose solutions. Author Budd Schulberg, who recently died at the age of 95, was quoted in the *New York Times* as saying, "In our daily lives we have to constantly rise up and meet challenges—and that is what sums up what's best." He went on to say, "What has helped me achieve success is the fact that I have always been a realist, paid attention to details, observed carefully what was going on and tried to capture things as they actually happened." This is a good lesson for organization leaders.

Summary

- Public image helps to secure public support and community sanction.
- Community attention and recognition are important for the effective operation of not-for-profits.
- Not-for-profits need to be more aggressive in use of their websites and other forms of communication with the public.
- Opportunities to inform the public of successes, achievements, and outcomes are important for both fundraising and developing a larger donor base.
- Volunteers should be considered part of the strategy for advancing the work and should receive proper recognition and attention.
- The CEO should play a significant role in outreach to media and ways to advance the organization's recognition.
- The CEO should understand his or her role as the agency's representative and effectively reach and communicate with print and broadcast media.
- Branding defines the perception of an organization's work and helps the public to identify with its mission.

Chapter 5

The Social Work Professional— Manager and CEO

L et's start with a bit of history. Social work, or social welfare, began in this country soon after its development. Our country's founders who came from England were highly individualistic, believed in self-determination and individual and personal responsibility, were churchgoing and very religious, and were distrustful of government based on their own British and European history. This distrust manifested itself in the motto, "No government is good government," and later on in "When the legislature is in session our rights are in peril." This strong family, church, and community orientation is known as the "Protestant ethic."

The origin of the ethic and strong belief system grew out of the Elizabethan Poor Laws of 1601, which defined the legal and community responsibility for caring for the poor, indigent, and indentured. These laws differentiated the "deserving poor" from the "undeserving poor." On one hand, the *deserving* poor were those who through no fault of their own were brain damaged at birth, missing a limb, disabled, or otherwise impaired. They were to be treated somewhat humanely and not shunned by their landholding employers. Although they were assisted, the deserving poor nevertheless lived under the stigma that their disability was a punishment delivered upon them by the Lord for a misdeed they or their forbearers committed.

The *undeserving* poor, on the other hand, were described as lazy, drunkards, derelicts, weak in mind, and usually not God-fearing. They were often removed from the community and placed in workhouses (sometimes referred to as "poorhouses" or "almshouses"). If they worked as demanded by the legal system, room and board were provided in a workhouse. If they refused to work, they were often imprisoned, deported, or in other ways removed from the community. While Darwin's experiments were still to come two centuries later, the Poor Laws were in fact the first application of Social Darwinism in Western culture. Survival of the fittest and natural selection were indeed the practice.

The Church, Immigration, and the Beginning of Social Services

These values and views of the biological and social status of human beings traveled across the seas and became firmly

embedded on U.S. soil. The church became the major supporter of services to the "poor and indigent." Over the years,
those who were blind, deaf, or otherwise infirm were treated
more humanely, although hardly as equals. Those who refused to work were viewed as undesirables as they had been
in England, and what today might be called genetically in-
ferior. So what did all of this mean for the beginning of the
field of social services?

First, as the colonies and then our newly emerged country
grew and developed, the Episcopal Church became the major
source of care to the needy. (Other religions also supported the
concept of tithing.) The church elders formed a committee
to determine who was deserving and then provided food or
shelter. If they believed that parents could not adequately care
for their children, the church established orphanages to house
them. This was the beginning of our fragmented system called
"child welfare," what is now known as "foster care."

The church essentially became the source of both provision and disposition on such issues as removal of children,
work relief, and assistance. As our country grew with large
numbers of poor immigrants and our Industrial Revolution
reached its zenith, the numbers of poor needing assistance
grew exponentially. The newcomers were at first from central
and southern Europe—Germans, Scandinavians, Northern
Italians—and later from Eastern Europe—Polish, Hungari-
ans, Russians, and of course large Jewish populations from
these countries. Jewish charities also arose to serve them. The
large numbers of Asians, particularly Chinese, brought over
to work on our expanding railroad system were excluded
from the system of privately run, church-supported services
to the poor. Over the years, the Chinese community developed its own system of services as did other Asian groups
who immigrated to the states. The European population was

primarily located in major cities like New York, Philadelphia, and Boston, where industry and manufacturing were expanding and jobs were plentiful. The conditions were abysmal; adults worked for long hours in sweatshops for pennies. Often two or three families shared one tenement apartment with bathroom facilities located on a floor serving many. Health care for the poor, other than in a few city hospitals and well-baby clinics, was nonexistent. Compulsory education was not yet a reality, so children were not obligated to attend school; many worked with their parents in sweatshops or begged on the streets. Most lived in dangerous, crime-ridden communities and often for their own survival formed what we now call street gangs. It is estimated that in the early 1850s, when New York's population was slightly over 700,000, there were as many as 10,000 homeless children and teens living by their own wits on the streets. The press referred to these children as "street Arabs" or "wayward waifs." Those who were not outright begging were bootblacks (shoeshine boys) or newspaper hawkers.

The outcasts were as young as seven or eight years of age. Older boys often took care of their younger friends and the lucky ones staked out sleeping quarters over the newly constructed subway tunnels, which generated heat from below, for winter comfort. There were also many young girls who were homeless because their parents could not house or feed them. These girls were referred to in the *New York Times* in the middle and late 1800s as "Singing Girls." They would wander down to the docks where the ships would be moored and sing for the sailors. Often the sailors would bring them aboard, abuse them, give them a few pennies, and take them back to shore. The young "prostitutes" were considered social outcasts; many contracted venereal diseases and wandered about untreated for a few years before their lives came to an end.

Some children were lucky and able to find outlets established by organizations like the Children's Aid Society (CAS). "Newsboys' houses," located in what is now lower Manhattan, charged the young "urchins" three pennies per night, which covered their room and board with one of the pennies establishing a savings account.

In the beginning, "social services" had a strong religious orientation based on the belief that "thriftiness was close to Godliness." Horatio Alger wrote many of his "rags-to-riches" tales by living among the boys in the newsboys' homes. Some became productive members of society by working as printers, tradesmen, masons, and shoemakers using skills they had learned in the newsboys' homes. Later these homes became "industrial schools," where thousands of boys and later girls were trained in skills needed by our ever-growing economy. Some also became teachers, doctors, and lawyers, but most of the training prepared these youngsters for work in our industrial and agricultural society.

The Friendly Visitors movement grew out of this period. Families that remained reasonably intact while living in uninhabitable tenements were viewed as "savable." Churches, largely through their women's auxiliaries developed a program that grew in size to become a movement referred to as the "Friendly Visitors Movement." Wealthy women volunteered through their church to visit poor families, establish relationships with the inhabitants, tidy up apartments, and provide some of the basic necessities while making a special effort to care for the children. Personal hygiene was one of the hallmarks of the program, assuring that the children would be clean and have regular baths so that they could, among other things, attend church on Sundays. Vitamin-deficiency diseases such as rickets were endemic and tuberculosis and other respiratory diseases including pneumonia were rampant and caused the deaths of many children in these poor neighborhoods.

The Friendly Visitors volunteers became a main force in poor neighborhoods, and while the volunteers helped mothers with childcare they also made efforts to keep children together with their parent or parents, thus reducing the number of homeless children who roamed the streets of the city. There was great concern in the newspapers and in city government that there were too many children wandering the streets of New York and creating a menace to law-abiding citizens.

The Social Services Profession Evolves

The Friendly Visitors movement, the newsboys' houses, the emergence of settlement houses serving the newly arrived immigrants, and some public hospitals were the beginning of what we know today as the *social services network*. All of these programs were privately sponsored and supported. There were little to no government funds directed toward these services. As time went on, the system could no longer handle the huge and complex needs of the poor. The volunteers were an insufficient labor force to sustain the programs. They often became board members and others were employed to do the actual work with families. CAS, Community Service Society, City Mission Society, the settlement houses, and later the Visiting Nurse Service provided employees to meet the ever-growing and more complicated needs of the poor. These were the early social workers, even though they were referred to as "agents," "counselors," or "youth workers." The profession of social work began to emerge from this history.

The settlement houses grew out of troubled and chaotic poor communities. The early days of social work were reformist in nature and settlement houses became the advocacy voice for the newcomer, the undereducated, and the poor. Almost all of them were located in poor neighborhoods. The first settlement house in New York and in the United States was the University Settlement located on Eldridge and Rivington streets on the Lower East Side and it still stands on the very spot where it was first created. The second was Hull House, founded by Jane Adams in Chicago, Illinois. Many other settlements dotted the landscape of the Lower East Side—the Henry Street Settlement, the Educational Alliance, the Grand Street Settlement, Hamilton Madison House, and a slew of others of smaller dimension. While the settlements welcomed the newcomer, offered English lessons, educated the children, provided summer camp vacations, and in many cases offered health and dental care, they also became the lobby for community action. The community used the settlement house both as a convening institution and a political lobby fighting for better housing, paved sidewalks, streetlights, and general improvement in living conditions.

Later they were active participants in establishing better working conditions for the poor, such as child labor laws, minimum-wage standards, and care for those injured on the job. They also pressured government for compulsory-education statutes and a variety of programs to protect children. The settlements were hubs of community activity and in many ways the central force in giving expression to the needs of the newly arrived Americans. In many cases, the predominant language of the settlement was that of the country of origin. One can find records of menus and programs in German, Italian, and Yiddish. The Educational Alliance, on lower Broadway in New York City, for example, offered kosher meals to those who requested them

The comprehensive program of the settlements offered direct service with a strong element of self-help and "mutual aid." Even in the late 1800s and early 1900s, the thinking was to offer citizens the right to self-determination, unionization, and political action. Many of the leaders in this reform effort became community activists or elected officials.

As mentioned earlier, other organizations emerged, each with its own flavor and service priority but together constituting a web of activity directed toward integrating the newcomer into the community, caring for the children, and providing services to the elderly. CAS had "industrial schools," which later became children's centers in many of the poor neighborhoods. CAS also created farm schools, year-round camps for unemployed teenagers, mother-and-children fresh-air programs, community mental-health clinics, and convalescent care for children suffering childhood diseases. The famous Orphan Train Movement, where abandoned New York City children were placed in homes out west, was also a feature of CAS. While these were the core programs of that organization, it was also during this period that CAS, in its more reform-minded state, advanced the concept of free kindergartens and dental services in schools, and was instrumental in creating the first child labor and compulsory-education laws. The admixture of services and advocacy for social and political reform was the hallmark of all of these "charities." Community Service Society, the City Mission Society, the Salvation Army, the Foundling Hospital, and later Catholic Charities were all part of the effort to provide a better life for the poor and a positive voice for change.

The profession of social work emerged out of the need to staff these institutions and understand the complex nature of the work. The first schools of social work were in New York and were called the Jewish School of Social Work and later the New York School of Social Work (now a part of Columbia University). Social work became the main professional instrumentality for change, community organization, and social advocacy. The main objective was to make life better for all, especially the poor and the needy, and to create a safer environment for children. In later years, as the African American population migrated north and west from the "black belt" states, programs all too slowly developed to serve the needs of those families. CAS was among the first to establish children's centers in Harlem, referred to as Utopia House and the Kennedy Center. The Harlem-based programs also helped in the development of a political infrastructure where partnerships were formed with the Urban League, Abyssinian Baptist Church, and a number of trade unions, especially the Brotherhood of Sleeping Car Porters under the leadership of A. Phillip Randolph.

While reform was central to the emerging social work profession, so was the influence of Freudian psychology. As the profession grew and as more schools of social work evolved they became disciples of this new and enticing psychological orientation. Community residents, once called "members" or "consumers," were now referred to as "clients." The social work curriculum became more and more psychological in orientation and at times was indistinguishable from the profession of psychology, especially clinical psychology. While social work maintained its *biopsychosocial* orientation, the *bio* and the *social* became the caboose and the *psycho* the engine. Caseworkers became the predominant professional group within social work and occupied roles in clinics, hospitals, and community institutions that featured counseling, adjustment services, and behavioral modification. As the not-for-profit world enlarged, so did the need for "clinically trained" workers while the need for reform-minded community organizers or group workers receded.

Schools of social work followed the marketplace and became more imbued with the clinical model. This was what the field seemed to want and what prospective students seemed interested in. It gave social work an identity and a body of knowledge that allowed the profession to grow and establish its place within the accredited, recognized, and sanctioned professions. Much of the work was excellent and over a period of time more social workers were practicing psychotherapy in agencies and in private practice than psychiatrists or clinical psychologists. Considering that social work was a professional latecomer, its growth was quite remarkable and in many ways eclipsed that of its older sister professions.

In the fifth edition of *The Social Worker as Manager*, by Robert Weinbach (Pearson Education Inc., 2008), the author states that social-work-trained clinicians also function in some measure as managers—that is to say, everyone performs some management functions, including supervision of subordinates, managing department budgets, and other administrative and management tasks. However, Weinbach indicates that there is much more to the role of manager than these specific functions and tasks, which many social workers find unpleasant and in some instances stressful. Stress goes with the territory of management and is compounded by the level of responsibility, size of the agency, and complexity of the decisions that need to be made.

We need to differentiate between management levels. A midlevel manager can indeed feel caught between lower-level staff and upper-level administrators. Without proper management and leadership training these individuals can often feel conflicting loyalties to their peers, supervisor, and organization. Of course, it is the responsibility of the mid-level manager to resolve conflicts in an impartial way that results in a positive outcome and increases worker productivity.

Managerial Roles in Social Services

Social workers who assume managerial roles also feel a loss of client contact. This is invariably the case where many social workers feel removed from the clients and distant from the personal satisfaction and rewards that accrue when clients do well and overcome obstacles. Once again, training in leadership helps social workers understand and deal with these feelings and redirect their need for satisfaction in ways that continue to give them a feeling of accomplishment even though the work may be multilateral and less personalized.

Finally, social workers are not trained to be comfortable with power. Social workers typically enter the profession because they are compassionate, kind, humanistic, and want to help and heal. They often feel they do not want or need to be in a position of authority and have the power to influence not only "feelings and behavior," but also work-related decisions that affect colleagues' status, jobs, and well-being. Power needs to be understood, grappled with, and integrated. Social workers at times have difficulty setting limits or saying "no" and would rather be seen as "yes" people. Managers must be comfortable saying "no," and should not feel responsible for someone else's unhappiness or guilty about outcomes.

Gender also affects attitudes toward power. One reason female social workers have avoided seeking higher-level management positions is they have been socialized into believing power is undesirable. Interestingly, while the field of social work is 75 percent female, less than 25 percent of the top managers are women. Women managers in all sectors of work have experienced the invidious dual definitions of either being fuzzy, soft, kind, nice, and compassionate (the traditional view of women) or tough, demanding, authoritative, and task-oriented. Interestingly men do not suffer the same negative work assessments. Men prefer to be seen as strong, no-nonsense, outcome or bottom-line driven, and performance oriented. It is generally assumed that women are more expressive and men more instrumental. But those roles assigned to gender are disappearing, albeit slowly. It is more likely than not that over the next 10 years, more women trained in leadership will be willing and of course able to assume the top positions in social agencies. Over the past several years, women in focus groups throughout the country have indicated they are capable of becoming CEOs of not-for-profits but believe that if they accepted the CEO position it would negatively affect their personal and family life. Long hours, child-care arrangements, and household responsibilities were listed as some of the compromising issues. But more significantly, many women did not want to be in a position of additional stress that often accompanies high-level management positions and did not feel comfortable dealing with male-dominated boards of directors. Many women in these focus groups expressed the view that men on boards who often represent the commercial and business world think that women are too emotional, soft, earthy, and touchy-feely and cannot make difficult and tough decisions. Though most of the women thought that was stereotypical, they did not wish to put themselves in the position of having to educate these men and at the same time run a social agency.

Carol Tosone, associate professor at NYU's Silver School of Social Work, in a 2009 article in the journal *Psychoanalytic*

Social Work, wrote, "Freud once described mental health as the ability to love and to work. For many of these women, their work also has to become their love, their passion. Working long hours, often working 'twice as hard as men,' to be viewed as equally competent, perhaps sacrificing spouse and children in deference to career, these women have been inculcated into a patriarchal corporate environment, one in which they must act in a sexual dissonant manner in order to succeed." This quote represents the dilemma: to conform to masculine norms of the corporate environment or to express your own sense of worth and style of caring. Women are struggling to reconcile these polarized expectations. This situation will change over the coming years as more women throughout our economy in both the for-profit and not-for-profit worlds assume greater positions of responsibility and leadership.

In the early 1960s, the Council on Social Work Education moved toward a "generic" curriculum. Graduate students in social work no longer selected a specialization such as casework, group work, community organization, administration, or research, but were trained with a knowledge base that reflects the full range of professional skills needed to practice. While the effort was to provide "generalists" to the field and respond to the marketplace needs, the effect was to further submerge community organization, group work, and administration, and elevate casework as represented by the clinical approach. Caseworkers were dominant, faculties were trained with a strong clinical background, and schools catered to an ever-growing number of applicants. There is a strong interconnection between the values of our larger society and the development of the profession of social work. When our political leadership no longer valued reform to better provide for those in need, fewer jobs became available for social workers. Institutions that were reform minded in their earlier days changed their direction and orientation, requiring more clinical practitioners and fewer community organizers and group workers.

The result of this change was institutionally very significant. As social workers became proficient clinically they were both less trained for and less interested in running the institutions in which they were employed. Their knowledge base, skill level, and orientation enabled them to work directly with clients and be helpful in adjustment services, but not to deal with important organizational and management issues. Over a period of years, social services organizations that were largely managed and led by social-work-trained professionals under the direction of reform-minded boards of directors slowly began to fade away. As the early leaders in social work grew older or retired, those who replaced them, while highly skilled, were trained in law, business, and education. Social workers became the clinical staff, and the managers of the institutions were from other disciplines and professions.

While this arrangement seemed acceptable, the long-term effect was a culture change. The initial mission of the agency as an institution for social change evaporated. More recently, many in the social work profession have recognized this disjunction and are now addressing the issue in ways that will again effectively position social workers to become the CEOs and management leaders of social services agencies.

Summary

- The origins of many organizations lie in the Elizabethan Poor Laws, which focused on services for the "deserving poor."

- Today's clients—substance abusers, domestic violence perpetrators and victims, school dropouts, and undocumented immigrants—are from populations that in the past would have been considered "undeserving poor."
- The social work profession grew out of early church movements such as Friendly Visitors and church-sponsored social services.
- The history of social work is found in the early settlement house movement, which had a reform orientation dedicated to serving the needy, the newcomer, and the poor.
- The reform movement of the social work profession began to shift in the middle of the twentieth century toward a more clinical and psychological orientation.
- Schools of social work need to focus greater attention on the environmental and social factors affecting clients in addition to concentrating on management and administrative skills required to lead social agencies.
- The preponderance of executives in not-for-profit agencies are male, while three-quarters of the workforce is made up of women; this must be addressed.
- The social work "generic curriculum," while providing graduate students with broad and general training, does not sufficiently offer the knowledge and skills needed for today's practice.
- Social work needs to develop a larger cadre of leaders who are trained and have the capacity and interest to become CEOs of social agencies.

Chapter 6

Programs and Priorities

A concise and clear mission statement defines what your organization does and helps the world around you, including boards, funders, government, and the public, understand what you are about and why you do it. Along with an orientation it is also an excellent educational piece for staff, who always need to know what the organization they work for is about. It is also a very good governor for executive leaders and board, providing parameters and direction, which prevents the organization from straying too far into another lane.

Creating an Effective Mission Statement

The public, of course, wants to know about the *who, what, when, where, why,* and *how* of an organization. For example: "The X, Y, and Z organization, founded in 1920, exists to help the children of parents who are or have been incarcerated. Governmental agencies refer children whose parents have been sentenced to prison terms and X, Y, and Z then determines whether they can be cared for by relatives or require other living arrangements such as foster care. X, Y, and Z continues to work with the children during the period of surrogate care and ensures that they receive a sound education and are in a safe and healthy environment. The organization also reaches out to the biological parent or parents and where appropriate arranges for visitation and later reunification. X, Y, and Z also assures the referring governmental agency that the children are well cared for and all of the legal requirements as determined by the court are met."

This mission statement is reasonably clear, defines the limits of the organization's involvement, and lets the public know how the organization will help the children and indirectly the family. The *who, what, when,* and *why* are reasonably answered. With respect to the *how,* the mission might state that trained caseworkers will do home visits, prison visits, and school visits, and arrange for a variety of family activities in keeping with the overall state of well-being for the children.

Does the mission statement leave anything out? Here's where the intersection between mission and vision needs elaboration. For example, what happens when X, Y, and Z has to place the children in another home? Do they have the responsibility to re-place the children? What is their advocacy role in the courts with respect to re-placement? Do they have the legal standing to appear before the court? Can they advocate for the children when they reach majority at age 18, and who assumes responsibility for them? What happens if the minor children commit delinquency or juvenile offender crimes and are sentenced? I could go on posing a variety of other questions that have to do with the expansion of the original mission based on new developments and events that require a change of position by the leadership of X, Y, and Z. In other words, the mission should never be static but rather broad enough to allow for an ongoing and dynamic interpretation of new needs relative to the X, Y, and Z role and function.

The problem for many organizations is that the mission remains locked in place for years, if not decades, which does not allow for a broader look at the needs of the clients as they change. The mission becomes a closed-in tube that at times doesn't reflect what the organization should be doing and in a strange way also protects the organization, which may fear stepping outside of what it knows and can do. Mission, therefore, can be a very positive statement of organizational direction or can be an imposed limitation on the organization's desire, ability, and capacity to be dynamic and reflect change as new needs arise.

How Changes in Vision Affect Your Mission

In recent years there have been many instances when not-for-profit organizations have expanded their original mission to address new and pressing needs. Organizations whose mission was to provide mental health counseling had to readjust their posture and priorities during the 1970s movement toward "deinstitutionalization." Tens of thousands of institutionalized patients were released in the 1970s when a national movement emerged that believed patients would do better living with their families or in communities. Whole new institutional arrangements developed where patients living in single-room-occupancy hotels were visited by mental health professionals and community agencies were enlisted to provide both the space and facilities to work with patients who were now residents in their service areas. Professionals who previously saw a patient by appointment in their office now had to make major adjustments in the way a mental health service was delivered. The concept of Community Mental Health developed during this period and organizations serving this population also needed to make substantial adjustments in their practice that required an enlargement of their mission.

The existence of large numbers of homeless people, especially families, was brought to the attention of not-for-profit agencies and the public in the mid-1980s. Before, there were some organizations, particularly "mission houses," usually sponsored by the Salvation Army or other church-related organizations, that served those who were "down and out." The mission houses in New York were usually in lower Manhattan around the Bowery and were viewed by the public as flophouses where rooms were very cheap and included meals. The 1980s, however, changed the public perception of the homeless, which now included large numbers of unemployed families. The Vera Foundation, under the leadership of Herb Sturz, was one of the first organizations to provide safe lodgings for homeless adults.

Affordable housing became almost nonexistent everywhere. Thousands of people were thrown out of their apartments, notably by eviction of the primary tenant, shutting down of dual or triple occupancy in public housing, housing abandonment by landlords in neighborhoods serving the poor, and rent gouging by landlords as a way to avoid rent stabilization laws. Agencies were faced with a new social landscape that included temporary shelters set up by municipal governments, often referred to as "transitional housing," or "welfare hotels." This arrangement was a response to the large numbers of people, including children, who were living in public parks, in abandoned subway tunnels, and on street corners.

Very few agencies had programs to serve this population and they needed to review their mission and their programs if they were to reach these estimated 40,000 to 50,000 people in New York City alone who were in a state of temporary or permanent homelessness.

Some agencies were able to make the transition with relative ease. Settlement houses, principally the Henry Street Settlement and organizations such as the Children's Aid Society (CAS), sponsored transitional housing for homeless families. These agencies assigned staff members to welfare hotels to work with families and set up health clinics, after-school and recreational programs, and summer camps. Many advocacy organizations emerged and some, like the Legal Aid Society, shifted gears to respond to this new urgent need.

However, there were many other not-for-profits that could have responded positively to this crisis but decided it was not within their mission to serve the new population. Some not-for-profits did shift program emphasis, without essentially changing their core identity, and chose not to live by the narrower definition found within their earlier mission. Clearly, some organizations were afraid to broaden their base, thinking that they would not be successful, that their board would not support their new efforts, or that the public would not understand their outreach. Once again, vision, leadership, and appropriate risk taking are keys to understanding not only an agency's direction, but also its actual survival. If agencies remain static, it is likely that they will eventually fall by the wayside.

Much can also be said about the period in the mid-1980s when crack cocaine and AIDS emerged as major social forces. Some agencies saw the problems, figured out how to be of assistance, shifted their program priorities, and without hesitation reached out to the new needy populations. Others did not.

Child welfare agencies moved to establish programs serving children suffering from AIDS, crack cocaine, and substance abuse and developed innovative partnerships with medical facilities. Agencies that relied on what they had done in the past and did not change were viewed as traditionalists and in many instances were not only left behind but in some cases actually de-funded. Agency leadership at both the board and the staff level requires an aggressive, progressive, and dynamic analysis of the changes in our environment and the ways in which the not-for-profit agency could and should respond.

Much can be written about the failures in our public school system, with 30 to 40 percent high school dropout rates, school violence at a high point, and school attendance at historically low figures. The *New York Times*, in an October 20, 2009, editorial, "Home Alone," took the position that after-school programs are a cost-effective way to boost student achievement, reduce juvenile crime, and help overstressed working parents. In the same editorial, the *Times*'s editor points out that "the most striking and disturbing finding of a recent study by the After School Alliance is the 15.1 million latchkey children left alone and unsupervised at the end of the regular school day. In that same study, 18.5 million parents say that they would enroll their children in an after-school program if one were available to them. The community need is clear."

Once again, social agency executives who were aware of the need took the position that it was not their problem or issue and thought solutions should be found only within the traditional and formal educational system. Others took the exact opposite approach, believing that education is everyone's business and that many of the issues and problems found in our public schools were not solely of an academic or instructional nature but rather the result of our social condition. There needed to be an examination of the circumstances surrounding the students and what they brought to the school situation. Did they come to school hungry? Were they abused or neglected? Did they live in doubled- or tripled-up housing? Were they not attending school because they had to watch a younger sibling? These and other questions related to issues of poverty, racism, and environment were issues that were more familiar to social agency professionals than to those in the formal educational system. Many not-for-profits sprang into action, joining with school districts to form full-service schools, community schools, health and mental-health clinics within the school building, and a variety of other programs. An expansion of mission reflecting the changed social condition and the capacity of agency leaders to broaden their mission allowed them to respond to the new need. This is what is meant by *visionary leadership*.

The Bureau of Labor Statistics of the U.S. government reported in November 2009 that our unemployment rate exceeded 10.2 percent, with the real number at 17.5 percent when it included people who were underemployed and those who had already ceased looking for work. Peter S. Goodman, in the article, "The Recession's Over, But Not the Layoffs," (*New York Times,* November 7, 2010) suggests that this condition might turn out to be structural and not go away as the economy improves. He says that manufacturing jobs have declined so sharply that in some instances they no longer exist and globalization has changed the nature of the world and U.S. economy. While each month we hope for better news, the jobless rate continues to be at the highest levels since the 1930s and most experts seem to agree that the number, especially for youth and nonwhite populations, will remain extraordinarily high for at least the next three to five years.

Here is the question for the not-for-profit world: What is the best role for nonprofits in this period of sluggish growth and slow recovery? Some agencies that traditionally rendered general employment counseling and job-finding services greatly expanded their role to include extensive job training and retraining, and opening up trainee positions in fields within the not-for-profits' world. These jobs are within industries typically related to the not-for-profit field and suggest intermediate and long-term growth potential for health care positions, preschool programs (assistant teachers and family workers), nutritionists, nursing home attendants, in-home hospice care workers, and other child-care-related positions. Once again the opportunity presents itself to agency leaders to redefine their work in broader, more necessary and visionary terms. Job counseling for jobs that no longer exist seems to be not only a waste of time but unhelpful to those we are meant to serve. Breaking out of an old and comfortable mode is needed, but not always easy to do.

Changing Direction

Of course, a change in an organization's direction requires careful examination of capacity, management, and budget. An organization that blindly grows without a clear and strategic understanding of what that growth entails makes an enormous error. Even when the organization's leadership understandably wants to address a critical issue, they also must plan for that in advance and make sure their house is in order. This involves more than rearranging the furniture; it requires:

- Ensuring full support of your board, redirection of internal resources, and careful examination of existing services to determine which ones are no longer relevant.
- Securing new resources from both the private and public sectors and developing a clear and concise message to your donor support network.
- Establishing an intensive short-term staff development and training program to provide the needed knowledge, skills, and tools that will enable participation in the agency's new programmatic direction.
- Establishing a modest evaluation component to assess periodic outcomes of the new direction, allowing for midcourse correction, and after a set period of time determining whether the new direction was worth the effort.

Any new direction or program initiative can bring with it problems and/or consequences that did not exist previously. Agency leaders need to overcome the fear of what might happen and, within reason, establish a damage-control policy to deal with the potential fallout that might occur. The damage-control system should be owned by the chief executive, the board, staff, outside legal counsel where appropriate, and where applicable, the agency's public information or public relations director. In other words, ownership of the new direction and possible negative consequences should be shared with key stakeholders. Press and media queries should be answered only by assigned staff who are familiar with the agency's positions.

Sound and effective damage control needs to be a professionally developed process, not a crisis-driven response. Leadership is important to a successful implementation plan. The leader must be calm, clear-minded, and willing to adapt quickly and creatively respond to new and unexpected circumstances. Should negative fallout occur, it is important to involve the team and conduct a programmatic postmortem to learn what went wrong.

Changing direction based on new social conditions should not be confused with the undisciplined pursuit of *more*. Jim Collins, in his book *How the Mighty Fall*, (HarperCollins, 2009) suggests that some leaders grow their organization in what he describes as five stages:

Stage 1: Hubris born of success

Stage 2: Undisciplined pursuit of more

Stage 3: Denial of risk and peril

Stage 4: Grasping for salvation

Stage 5: Capitulation to irrelevance or death

Some leaders "grow their organizations not in response to need or vision, but out of a sense of personal glorification and can take the organization down the path of destruction. We have seen this many times. Organizations fail because they had a 'leap growth' philosophy unrelated to consumer demand, internal capacity and sustainability. Leaders sometimes see this as the counterpoint to complacency and lack of innovation but in fact what they are doing is more dangerous than maintaining the status quo. The leaders in our industry should not be obsessed with growth, but rather sensitive to the need for change which may require redirection or in some cases growth within manageable limits."

Douglass C. Eadie, in his article "Building the Capacity to Lead Innovation," in the book *Effectively Managing Non-profit Organizations* (NASW Press, 2006), suggests a number of key steps with respect to the leadership and management process. Develop a clear, detailed strategic framework that includes what the direction aspires to achieve, key roles and functions, and the values and the ethical framework embodied in the plan. Establish rational priorities, the reasons for changing an organization's direction, and the opportunities that it presents. Develop a comprehensive and balanced approach. How does the change affect existing program revenue resources, customers, clients, governance, and stakeholder relationships? What is the wisdom of taking a high-risk course of action and what is hoped to be gained by establishing this direction? Have realistic expectations—expect success but be prepared for falling short.

Summary

- A clear and definable mission statement, understood by the board, the staff, funders, and the public is absolutely essential.
- The vision of an organization needs to intersect with its mission. The vision can be a larger statement dealing with current and future needs.
- Advocacy by an organization in addition to provision of services needs a clear statement for public recognition and understanding.
- Mission should never be so finite that it doesn't allow for change.
- Opportunities exist for all not-for-profits to expand their mission and deliver a needed service.

- In the current economic climate, not-for-profits should be aware of and concerned about issues affecting the general population, such as job security, health insurance, and economic stress.
- Change requires an organization to carefully examine its capacity, management structure, and budget.
- The governing board needs to be involved, along with the chief executive, in making key decisions that effect organizational change.
- Agency leaders need to overcome the fear of change. Damage-control and crisis-management strategies should be developed by all not-for-profits.

Chapter 7

Public Policy and Government Relations

All not-for-profits must be conscious of their public image. Organizations want to be viewed as responsible, reliable, fiscally prudent, honest, and transparent. Not-for-profits that engage or interface with governmental agencies have an additional burden because some may function as both a critic of governmental policy and a supporter of governmental initiatives. A good example is the issue of universal health insurance, where many not-for-profits have been justifiably critical of government for not covering more citizens while at the same time being supportive of recent governmental initiatives to expand coverage to the uncovered. The crisscrossing role of critic and supporter gives organizational leaders professional agita and executive headaches. It is even more difficult for those not-for-profits that accept governmental grants, contracts, or subsidies and in good measure exist because of contractual arrangements such as foster care, adoption, after-school programs, and juvenile justice.

Bridging the Gap between Independence and Advocacy

How does an organization maintain its independence, autonomy, right to advocate, and responsibility to advance a cause on behalf of its clients when it is also receiving substantial sums of money from the very source it is criticizing? This seems like an unsolvable conflict and dilemma. Many not-for-profits have chosen to lower their profile, stay under the radar, and not take public positions. Others committed to the social policy and advocacy functions have elected not to accept government dollars for specific services, so they do not face the conflict. I am not referring to the 501(c)3s that are the traditional think tanks (e.g., Urban Institute, Hastings Institute, Brookings Institution, Heritage) but to not-for-profits that had at one time accepted government funds and were in the direct-service business but were also advocates. The Community Service Society in New York is a prime example of an organization that chose the advocacy route because it was the more important function, and was willing to give up substantial sums of government money and shift internal priorities.

Other organizations have attempted to bridge this great divide differently. As an example, Children's Aid Society (CAS) continued its direct-service function without abandoning its public policy and advocacy posture. The organization recognized the dilemma but believed strongly that its reputation, past history, and accomplishments allowed it to continue in both functions without penalty. It accepted substantial dollars to deliver foster care services and at the same time was critical of government with respect to cutbacks in foster care payments, cutbacks in service, increased caseload size, and reductions in after-care. It believed itself strong enough and well positioned within the social and political structure of the city to withstand any penalty. CAS leaders learned that as long as their criticism was constructive and not personalized or politicized, governmental officials, more often than not, would understand and accept the duality. Organizations need to carefully assess their role within the social services system and their influence when making a decision. It is a delicate balancing act and requires analysis of alternatives and a damage-control plan should an unanticipated negative impact result.

Many not-for-profits have chosen another avenue. While not forfeiting their right to speak out on behalf of their clients or on issues that affect their constituents, they have lifted their voice in partnership with others, rather than in singular fashion. Throughout our country, convening and public policy coalitions exist that are made up of many agencies, either within or across a variety of fields of practice. They speak on behalf of the industry they represent. For example, agencies that provide child-care services or those in the geriatric or nursing home fields are able to speak with a united voice.

These organizations are not direct-service providers. They may or may not have tax-exempt status and in many instances the coalition is officially registered as a lobbyist. While these organizations or coalitions serve as trade associations seeking higher salaries and better working conditions, they also address the larger issues affecting clients, such as expansion of entitlement programs, eligibility requirements, and access to services. The agencies that join the coalition are therefore protected from being individually singled out and have dispatched their larger responsibility to speak to the issues of great importance.

Needless to say, executive leaders must insure that their board and/or organizational policymakers are fully aware of their membership in the coalition. There should be no surprises. Board members should not learn of the membership or public position that the coalition has taken in their local newspaper. Internal and external communication is the key to sound management, with transparency being central to the process. Being a member of a larger coalition offers some protection but should not be used as a smokescreen to hide behind. Although there is strength in numbers, organizations should not avoid taking a public position and merely hide behind anonymity.

Essential Steps to Being an Advocate

Laying the foundation to achieve sound advocacy results is an important function for leaders of organizations. Emily D. Pelton and Richard E. Baznik, in their article "Managing Public Policy and Government Relations" in *Effectively Managing Nonprofit Organizations* (NASW Press, 2006) suggest a number of steps to achieving a balanced public policy position:

- Map organizational resources and positions.
- Identify research and analyze the public issues.

- Understand the relevant policy and political processes.
- Get to know the public policy players.
- Get to know the sector players.

These are the most essential steps for organizational leaders as they position their agency as an advocate. The work always depends on the experience and quality of the professionals assigned to the advocacy function and of course, the resources available. It is counterproductive for professionals who have clinical and service experience but little in the policy arena to try to achieve positive public policy results. The functions are too important to do on the cheap and the skills needed to be an advocate are often quite different than those required of a good practitioner. Some organizations, trying to stretch their budgets, have asked staff with a particular set of skills to move into a different area of work in which they have had little or no training. Reassigning staff to the public policy function when they are ill prepared is detrimental. A training program for interested staff in the public policy functions is worth considering and can tap the resources of the staff more effectively. An organization needs to commit internal resources if it desires a meaningful public policy function. Research staff might be needed to provide direction or evaluation in addition to the staff who provide political knowledge and context.

Advocacy and Politics—Do They Mix?

After there is agreement on a clear public policy position and transparency within an organization's staff and governance group, the next decision is informing stakeholders and the public at large. How information is disseminated and the connection made to the organization's mission is critical. For example, an organization that has been engaged in pregnancy prevention education programs will in all likelihood be better understood if the organization takes a public position supporting Medicaid payments for abortions. The connection is clear and public support is more likely to be forthcoming. Some, no doubt, would not agree with the position but nevertheless it is still a logical extension of the organization's mission. The larger mistake is when an agency does not inform the community of the position that it is advocating.

Not-for-profits have been very concerned about their right to be advocates; much misinformation exists. Many misunderstand the law and believe that if the organization is tax exempt it cannot be an advocate. As long as an organization does not support specific candidates or politicize its position it can both provide education and serve as an advocate. The difference between advocating for candidates or political parties and advocating on relevant issues needs to be better understood by agency boards and executives.

Some hints will help:

- Be open and transparent and explain your position internally and externally with clarity and passion.
- Ask for support of other publics and/or organizations.
- Determine who your allies are and whether you wish to align yourself with them on a particular issue.
- Determine whether media support is available to your organization on that specific issue.
- Use or develop your relationship with decision makers and/or public officials who can be influential with respect to advancing the issue while protecting your agency.

Deciding what to advocate for and when is important. Developing a strong advocacy action plan with board member involvement is essential. The organization must have internal support prior to the taking of a public position. In their recently published book, *Forces for Good: The Six Practices of High Impact Not-for-Profits* (Jossey-Bass, 2007), Leslie R. Crutchfield and Heather McLeod Grant suggest that combining services with advocacy can have a powerful and positive impact. Organizations that have earned strong marks as service providers and have lifted themselves above the fray can have greater impact on policy than those that are viewed purely as "lobbyists." Crutchfield and Grant suggest that there is a connection between direct service and policy advocacy and within its circle there are grassroots support, service credibility, and channels for implementing change. Organizations can also change their service programs while engaging in advocacy as they discover new ways to better serve clients and achieve their goals.

Transformational change is never easy to achieve within a highly structured social system. Yet, when we look over the past half century we see that those with vision and strategic thinking, who utilize team building with clear purpose, indeed achieved major transformative change. Social Security, Medicare, Child Health Plus, and, going back even further, child labor and compulsory education laws were all the result of public policy initiatives that resulted in transformational change. More recently, the efforts to effectively redesign public education to create full-service and community schools and health and mental-health clinics within these institutions have all been equally transformative. We do have the capacity to influence the direction of our country and in so doing provide a better life for everyone.

Lack of health insurance kills about 45,000 Americans per year, according to a Harvard study released in September 2009. Who are these Americans who die for lack of insurance?

The study indicates that they are often single mothers who work hard, sometimes at two jobs, but are uninsured (many with children who are not receiving prenatal or pediatric care), or adolescent girls who die because they don't have a Pap smear even after suffering abdominal pain because they know that they cannot pay the doctor bills. Women who die of cervical cancer are almost always poor and their deaths can certainly be avoided if health care is provided. The Harvard study suggested that a woman dies in America every 12 minutes because she does not have health insurance that would have allowed her to see a physician or visit a health-care institution. This is certainly an issue that not-for-profits need to unite around to advocate for corrective legislation.

The not-for-profit field has a great opportunity to give attention to the high unemployment rate of unmarried women who are the heads of households. The Center for American Progress estimates that there are 1.3 million women who fall into this category. The effort to put Americans back to work requires prioritization of those segments of our population that need special attention. The unemployment rate for black Americans is 15.7 percent and even worse for black teenagers and young adults at 35 percent. Clearly we need to rethink our approach to employment and devote our policy and service objectives to those in the greatest need.

A recent survey by the Policy Institute (Center for American Progress) suggests that 1 in 4 families in the United States were hit by a job loss in 2008/2009. The not-for-profit sector can help to address this enormous issue in transformative ways much like the way our predecessors created the Civilian Conservation Corps (CCC), Works Projects Administration (WPA), and National Youth Administration (NYA). We have the capacity and opportunity to add hundreds of thousands, if not millions of people, to our industry. We can develop extensive job training programs and internships that can increase our capacity to serve families with expanded preschool programs, after-school services, summer camps, summer jobs for teens, and entry-level positions of all kinds. It is estimated that the not-for-profit sector now employs in excess of 20 million people. How difficult would it be to secure the funds to add an additional 2 million people to our ranks?

Summary

- There is a clear interface between governmental agencies and not-for-profits.
- Organizations that receive government funds need to be responsible and accountable but also maintain autonomy and independence.
- Advocating against government decisions is acceptable as long as the tax-exempt organization does not advocate for specific candidates or political parties.
- It is perfectly acceptable to combine service delivery with the larger functions of advocacy if it is related to the agency's mission.
- Some organizations have chosen not to accept government funds for fear of losing the right to be critical of government policy.
- Not-for-profits can express their public positions through umbrella organizations and coalitions.
- Developing partnerships can have a very positive effect on advancing positions shared by organizations of similar beliefs.
- CEOs should be careful to involve key board and staff before policy positions are made public.

- Achieving sound advocacy results requires careful articulation and strategy.
- All positions advanced by a not-for-profit should be transparent and available to key stakeholders.
- Organizations need not be lobbyists in order to be advocates.

Chapter 8

Lessons in Leadership

What makes a leader? Clearly a leader is one who has followers regardless of setting or station. Nonprofit leaders are no less decisive than business leaders. Leaders who fail to grasp the complex governance and power structures limit their ability to lead.

What Makes an Effective Leader?

An effective leader mobilizes and catalyzes commitment to a vigorous pursuit of a clear and compelling vision and stimulates higher performance standards. Differentiating the leader from a competent manager is difficult. A good manager organizes people and resources toward the efficient and effective pursuit of objectives. The manager is an organizer and implementer but not necessarily a catalyst or visionary. Obviously we can identify some leaders who are both, but that is the exception and not the rule. The leader helps build an institution from good to great. There is no single defining action, no one silver bullet, and no solitary lucky break that makes a leader great. Rather, the great leader is one who advances ideas, keeps pushing with persistent effort in an intelligent and consistent direction, and creatively uses his or her team until the objective is reached.

The executive director (ED) or chief executive officer (CEO) is the central person who inspires the not-for-profit organization, educates the board, builds the team, defines the objectives, refines the mission, and evaluates the results. The CEO is also the main force who establishes "the culture" of the agency, the values, and the mores and standards that surround it. The CEO needs to be intellectually curious and knowledgeable about ideas, research, and studies that affect the work of the organization.

Obviously, CEOs need to be people of vision who can think big, move the organization beyond its present state, and help merge vision with the organization's mission. They need to have a deep commitment and passion, not just for the organization, but for the clients served. They need to strive for excellence and hold the bar high for those they lead. CEOs need to be humble, and allow for openness, self-criticism, and self-reflection. Leadership requires sound communication skills and the ability to express emotion when facing issues of significance, passion, and indignation where appropriate. Leaders need to understand the behavior of individual employees and clients, motivate staff, create a learning environment, give credit to others, and show a willingness to invent and experiment.

All of these qualities are required for a leader to be successful and not just a vertical or top-down manager. Building a team requires understanding that horizontal inclusion does not diminish the leader's ability to be decisive, but rather adds to the team's sense of inclusion.

In *BusinessWeek*'s October 23, 2009 article, "Myths That Undermine Decision Making," author Bob Frisch examines a series of myths that are important and vital to the exercise of sound leadership:

- *Myth*: A single team can make all of the big decisions.

  Exploding the myth: There is no rarified group that knows everything. Depending on the issue, key people, including the CFO, the head of HR, the head of IT, and line staff, may constitute the right team to address a given issue.

- *Myth*: The executive team is a body of equals.

  Exploding the myth: Some members of the team might believe that they have the same decision rights as higher level executives. At times we inadvertently assist in this misconception. Some people, including the CEO, clearly carry more weight than others and ultimately are most accountable for the decision and its consequences. We need to be clear with all of the players from the beginning—what their roles are and whether their participation is advisory.

- *Myth*: Team members should always adopt a CEO perspective.

  Exploding the myth: Many CEOs expect team members who have wisdom and knowledge to lay aside their own ideas and adopt what they think the CEO wants.

Asking everyone to think like the CEO is clearly counterproductive and in no way adds to the process or the
outcome of sound decisions.

By addressing these myths Frisch suggests CEOs build
a formalized and flexible range of decision-making environ-
ments. They can then use the full power of their position
to advance the decisions of the group and hold themselves
accountable.

The Adaptive Leader

Leaders in our sector need to be adaptive. The environment
in which we live and work is one where crisis exists almost
continuously (job losses, homelessness, depression, teen sui-
cide, school violence, etc.). A leader cannot hunker down
and wait for the crisis to pass. Adaptive leaders know how to
seize an opportunity and in a sense hit the organization's reset
button. They use the turbulence of the present to build on
and bring closure to the past. In the process they may change
key rules of the game, reshape parts of the organization, and
redefine the work required of their staff.

Adaptive leaders need to make targeted modifications in
the organizational DNA, change some positions, and eliminate some jobs and redirect others. When tasks no longer
fit the new direction, then team members and sometimes
loyal colleagues whose work no longer is applicable must
be relieved of their assignment. Obviously, a leader must
have empathy for those who no longer fit the organization's direction or model and must rally colleagues to approach the new work tasks and strategies. It is important for
the leader to be able to distinguish the essential from the

expendable, not an easy task. The leader must be able to orchestrate the inevitable conflict, chaos, and confusion that an organization's change may bring so that the disturbance is productive.

In an article in the *Harvard Business Review*, William W. George refers to the "7 Lessons for Navigating the Storm":

1. Face reality, starting with yourself.
2. Don't be Atlas: Get the world off your shoulders.
3. Dig deep for the root cause.
4. Get ready for the long haul.
5. Never waste a good crisis.
6. You are in the spotlight: Follow your true beliefs.
7. Go on the offensive: Focus on winning now.

George indicates that "everyone inside the organization is watching what you do and it is imperative that the leader stay focused and set a standard for internally principled behavior" that will make the organization stronger.

The seven lessons are self-explanatory, so I will merely add a few comments. All leaders make mistakes, especially under great pressure. The key to being successful is openness, admitting mistakes, not being defensive, and being ready to make midcourse corrections and move forward. We have all learned that the problems we face rarely yield to quick-fix solutions; there is no vaccine or immunization to deal with the social problems at hand. We must be ready for the long haul. Finally, we should use any current crisis that the public is conscious of (i.e., public school failure) to move our organizations and their stakeholders forward to a new level of thinking and action. This is what is meant by viewing a crisis as an opportunity.

What Makes Leaders Successful?

Raymond T. Yeh, in the December 2005 issue of *Executive Association* (the journal of the New York Society of Association Executives), makes some very interesting observations. Leaders who are "dreamers" are disparaged until we realize they are visionaries who we then hold in high esteem. The point is that we shouldn't get hung up on terms, but rather look at the essential qualities of leadership. Leaders know that they need other people to help in achieving their dream and that when their best is called upon, they can deliver.

In that same journal, Barton Goldsmith addresses the tools that leaders need in order to be successful:

- A simple thank-you note or a birthday card goes a long way. More importantly, however, writing, whether essays, articles, or keeping thoughts in a log or diary, is a valuable reflective process that leads to self-discovery.
- Understand the importance of emotions. Feelings are a part of daily life and are often ignored by leaders.
- Have passion. A strong belief in what you're doing will fire up your colleagues.
- Communicate and listen. Both are important skills that too many of us ignore.
- Be a mentor to subordinates, particularly younger colleagues.
- Self-evaluate and share with colleagues. "What do we need to change?" "What do we need to learn?"
- Face fear, particularly that of team members who might be concerned about their livelihood.
- Don't fear failure; use mistakes as opportunities to learn what not to do.

- Have fun—it makes the job special and satisfying and increases productivity. Find ways of making it fun for others.

In the November 1, 2009 issue of the *New York Times*, Drew Gilpin Faust, president of Harvard University, said with respect to change that at the University of Pennsylvania, where she had been chair of a department and spent many years, she developed a strong loyalty and attachment to the place and the people. That loyalty, she suggests, made it difficult to advance needed changes because she was a part of what was. The lesson is that leaders must be self-conscious and detach themselves from past or current allegiances to allow themselves to see new issues and horizons for change. Faust, in the same article, also writes that people impute all kinds of things to leaders, sometimes thinking of them as disproportionately powerful and imagining them to be much more transcendent than they actually are. She suggests that it is important that colleagues and subordinates see that there really is no special mystery about what the leader is up to.

The Role of the Manager

Let us turn our attention to the role of manager, as differentiated from the role of leader. In separating the roles and functions of leadership from management, we have relegated the manager to the subordinate role of the bureaucrat who is less creative and imaginative, at times feared, and often not respected. A recent article in *Business Source Premier* states that "nobody aspires to be a good manager anymore; everyone wants to be a great leader."

Managers are absolutely essential within any organizational structure. The manager often gets the job done, organizes the teams, sets up the expectations, reviews the outcomes, and reports directly to the CEO.

Managers need to be collaborative, but also in charge and able to maintain order. In business, the manager must "make the numbers" while at the same time being nurturing and inclusive. Leaders must understand the value of managers, encourage them, and where possible elevate their roles within the workplace. Managers need to be analytical, know how to hold people accountable, understand that change is a constant factor, adjust the systems, and not resist new ideas even though they may require new metrics. Most importantly, good managers must also manage relationships up as well as down with all staff, colleagues, and partners.

Summary

- Leaders in the not-for-profit field need to be as decisive as business or government leaders, mobilize their troops to be a catalytic force, and understand the existing power structure.
- Leaders can be effective managers but a good manager is not necessarily an effective leader.
- Leaders need to be persons of vision who can think big, influence others, and help find new opportunities.
- Leaders know how to build a team and accept both top-down and bottom-up contributions.
- Leaders need to understand that the final and ultimate decisions rest with them or their board.
- Leaders need to be adaptive, understand the changing environment, and be able to reasonably predict future direction.

- Leaders need to understand how change affects people and develop strategic models that create opportunities and reduce the possibility of harm.
- Leaders need to understand that their actions and behavior are signals to others within the organization.
- Leaders need to understand their own limitations and be conscious of their own health and peace of mind.

Chapter 9

The Board and the CEO

The CEO and his or her top managers are the principal players who must be concerned about the process of establishing organizational goals, assuring continuity, reviewing practices and outcomes, and delivering on the organization's purposes and promises. The governing board is the organization's most important volunteer entity. An effective, involved, and supportive board is essential for an organization's long-term stability and success.

The Board of Directors

The members of the governing board (called *trustees*, *directors*, or in universities, *overseers*) are those whom the community has entrusted with the authority to serve as fiduciaries and policymakers. The board's principal function is to ensure that the organization is true to its mission, and its main responsibility is to hire the top professional, often referred to as the *CEO*, *president*, or *executive director*. The board's responsibility is to annually evaluate the CEO's performance by establishing performance guidelines and compensation arrangements. The board, together with the CEO, develops the organization's short- and long-range priorities and fiscal management structure, and ensures that all legal and ethical responsibilities are fulfilled.

The board is the central focus of power and legitimacy of the organization. Professionals, including the CEO, are mobile, often assuming other positions outside the organization, and are therefore not considered permanent players. The board, however, remains the main source of stability and continuity.

Another central obligation of the board is to establish criteria for selecting new board members through a defined, well-functioning, and active nominating committee. The committee must assure that nominations are impartial, representative, and reflective of diversity and do not cater to special interests. All board members should enjoy the prestige of the broader community, be able to contribute to the organization's mission, and give or raise funds to ensure that the organization achieves its programmatic objectives. In *Effectively Managing Nonprofit Organizations* (NASW Press, 2006), edited by Richard L. Edwards and John A. Yankey, the authors identify a number of key characteristics of effective boards:

- They learn the organization's values, norms, and traditions.
- They understand the agency's mission and purpose as differentiated from its competitors.
- They have respect for the professional leadership.
- They put aside their own individual interests and needs to achieve the larger goals of the organization.

Effective board members need to continually learn about the organization's changing programs and roles and self-reflect on their personal participation and contributions. Another important function of the board and one too often overlooked is their responsibility, together with the top professional managers, to review the agency's status and engage in strategic planning. Too many agencies have learned to live comfortably with the status quo, believing that what they have done in the past is sufficient for the present or future. Unless there is a mechanism within the organization to periodically review mission and programmatic direction, the organization can remain static and operate, at best, on inertia. In some organizations the board often waits for the CEO to initiate discussions related to programmatic or policy change while the CEO similarly waits for direction from the board. To avoid this, a mechanism must be in place so that the professionals, including the CEO and board members, have an opportunity and obligation to periodically engage in strategic analysis. Such analysis will help to determine whether the organization is effectively addressing current needs and securing sufficient data to permit a careful look at future direction. Today, not-for-profits, depending on their field of practice, should be analyzing whether they are effectively serving the new immigrant populations that exist throughout our country, or dealing with the fallout effects of the recent recession on individuals and families, or addressing the organization's position with respect to the racial divide in general and in their community of service.

The board also needs to periodically review its own collective performance and the performance of the individual members. Once on the board, a member should not have a lifetime appointment. Whether or not there are term limits, a review of each board member's contribution, attendance, committee assignments, and actions should take place periodically. Board education should be an ongoing function and not take place at just an annual or semiannual retreat. The CEO as well as the board chair has the primary responsibility for providing ongoing board education and development. Many have found that a program report by different agency supervisors and line staff at each board meeting is a valued part of board education. Arranging for field visits by members to different programs and installations makes good sense and gives them a direct, observable experience in operations.

In some instances it is perfectly acceptable for board members to be invited to sit in at agency staff meetings, seminars, and even case conferences, as long as confidentiality is maintained. Some not-for-profits have encouraged board members to enroll in university-based programs that feature courses in philanthropy, board governance, and social responsibility, which members have found valuable. Board teamwork and cohesion are central to the effective functioning of a board. Members who are not committed to a positive process can serve, even unwittingly, as unconstructive members. Some agencies have become hopelessly divided when individual board members unconsciously play a negative role in preventing board cohesion and unity. Weeding out these individuals should not be the sole responsibility of the CEO, although he or she should participate actively with the board nominating committee to identify recalcitrant members and find appropriate ways for them to leave the board.

The CEO

CEOs can no longer take the position, "Keep them in the dark, so that they'll leave you alone." Strong CEOs realize that their boards can be their best and most lasting partners. The CEO must be committed to board education, involvement, and true partnership. The same is true for the board, which must recognize that the CEO is not just a passive follower or compliant manager, but rather a true partner and leader who is the agency's main captain and implementer. The history of social agencies has often placed greater esteem on the board member or volunteer than on the professional. This is changing, however; the CEO, in most instances, has earned his or her stripes and demonstrated professional knowledge and acumen in leading and growing the organization.

In one instance, the board of an agency involved in serving children became understandably concerned and frightened after reading about corporate mismanagement in the for-profit world. The board asked the CEO about the limits of the agency's directors and officer's insurance. Several board members wanted to know whether they were sufficiently protected as a board and as individual members. The CEO provided the information they requested but failed to use the opportunity to educate the board on the greater risks inherent in dealing with children who were chronically ill, physically and psychologically damaged, and severely depressed.

The not-for-profit CEO has the knowledge, training, education, skills, and abilities that adequately correspond to those leaders in the for-profit world. If the leaders of not-for-profits do not possess vision, interpersonal skills, sound management capacity, and strong sense of self, they shouldn't be in the position as head of the organization. In today's not-for-profits the CEO is not only the principal spokesperson for the organization, but also the chief government relations officer, fundraiser, and recruiter. CEOs need to be clearheaded administrators who while being "yes" people are also comfortable saying "no," who know how to manage and lead, and who are committed, caring, and principled.

The not-for-profit sector has learned that its leadership and management style needs to be sufficiently differentiated from the corporate for-profit sector. While similarities exist with respect to executive leadership and board oversight, the not-for-profit executive needs to be a highly ethical person (particularly since we are often held to a higher standard) who understands that the bottom line is sound service delivery and advocacy promotion. Bending to self-serving considerations is unacceptable. Jim Collins, in *How the Mighty Fall* (HarperCollins, 2009), characterizes those in organizations who lose touch and are on the way down:

- People who shield those in power from grim facts, fearing penalty and criticism.
- People who assert strong opinions without evidence, data, or even a solid argument.
- People who prevent others from critical input or acquiesce to a wrongful decision.
- Leaders who seek all the credit and thus do not enjoy the confidence and admiration of their colleagues.

- Leaders who want to look smart or improve their own interests rather than do what's best for the overall team.
- Leaders who conduct autopsies filled with blame, seeking culprits rather than wisdom.

Successful leaders are those who share harsh realities, bring data and evidence to the table, respect challenging colleagues, unify behind the group decision, give and distribute credit to others, and enjoy healthy debate.

Leaders need to be more than consensus builders. They seek to make the right decisions regardless of how difficult and painful. The function of leadership is not dependent on popularity. Good leaders can build a team, forge consensus, not be fearful, take appropriate risks, make decisions based upon data and evidence, and then, when necessary, be prepared to stand alone.

Good leaders recruit and train subordinates in the organization's core values, manage and motivate staff, reward those who complete their tasks, are passionate in representing the organization, and have a level of maturity to effectively deal with crises.

The CEO must also be a network leader in order to achieve success. In the policy arena, not-for-profit leaders must see themselves as part of a larger network. In *Forces for Good: The Six Practices of High Impact Not-for-Profits* (Jossey-Bass, 2007), Crutchfield and Grant suggest that high-impact not-for-profits find other related organizations and establish formal or informal affiliations. Collaborative efforts to share resources allow the organization to have a larger public presence and influence. They also share knowledge and expertise with each other and effectively use the research, publications, replications, and pilots that others within the network have already established. Leaders can also draw upon a pool of talent that can be shared between organizations and encourage mobility of staff who are ready to move up the ladder. Professional leaders help build the coalitions, mobilize their collective force, and work for the common good.

Going your own way, while easier, is often not the best way to achieve long-term results. Being part of a network, coalition, or partnership often creates greater opportunity for leveraging influence and achieving shared goals and objectives.

Summary

- The governing board is the organization's most important volunteer entity.
- The board's main responsibility is to hire the CEO and evaluate his or her performance; board members must also understand their legal and moral responsibilities.
- The board establishes the legal standing for the organization that allows for its tax-exempt status.
- The board's other functions include selecting new board members, ensuring fiscal responsibility, and raising funds.
- Effective boards are those that understand the role, function, and programs of the organization and are knowledgeable about deliverable services.
- The board's relationship to the CEO needs to be one of mutual respect and shared vision.
- Boards should evaluate their own collective performance as well as the performance of individual members.
- The CEO should understand that he or she is responsible for board education and leadership development.
- The CEO plays a central role in organizational development.

- Leaders are consensus builders but also create opportunities for new and creative thinking.
- Effective CEOs are leaders not only in their own organization but in the field or profession of which they are a part.

Chapter 10

Raising Money, Managing Budgets, Building Relationships, and Thinking Ahead

Years ago, fundraising, referred to as *development*, was the province of the board of directors. The board members or trustees tended to be wealthy, philanthropic people who had social networks made up of important business leaders and decision makers. They took charge of the finances of the not-for-profit and understood their role as "giving, getting, or getting off." When the work of the organization became more complicated and when the dollar needs of the organization multiplied, the board often hired a professional fundraiser, often referred to as the "director of development." Over the past three or four decades, the development director assumed the major responsibility for bringing funds into the organization. The director worked closely with board members and continued to utilize board contacts, but the professional fundraiser became the main player in the organization's financial life.

Professional fundraisers, largely trained in organizations like the United Way of America, Red Cross, Salvation Army, and Faith-Based Federations, were knowledgeable about approaches to individuals, prospect mailings, donor solicitation, and more recently, charitable remainder trusts, mini trusts, rabbi trusts, and other deferred-giving instruments. They also understood the value of working with bank and insurance trust officers in directing bequests to the not-for-profit. Many older not-for-profits developed endowments or reserve funds gathered from bequests. Universities, medical centers, and large cultural organizations were and remain the main recipients of this type of giving.

Over the years, the structure and composition of boards of directors changed. While many are still comprised of the wealthy, it is no longer an exclusive club. Boards needed to change with the times and reflect the community at large, including alumni, parents, and in some instances government officials. While these changes were a step toward democratizing the governance process, the move to greater openness did diminish the board's capacity to support the organization's financial life. Simply put, boards were no longer made up of just the rich.

Enter the executive director or chief executive officer (CEO). The CEO needed to be concerned about the program, service, staff, and the client. Now he or she needed to work with the board on fundraising but also, depending upon the size of the not-for-profit, supervise the director of development. Some CEOs were comfortable in this new role while others got stuck. Did they want to be involved with fundraising and did they feel knowledgeable and comfortable? Did they have the time to devote to outreach and solicitation of funds? Did they feel they were given the authority to supervise the directors of development? Often the director of development was hired by the board and treated as an equal with the CEO. Sometimes, the director of development reported to the CEO and the board, which at times created some jurisdictional issues. In most instances it is far better for the director of development to receive direction and supervision from the CEO where both work closely with the board and its respective fundraising committees. The director of development should clearly know not only that he or she reports to the CEO but that his or her performance is also evaluated by the CEO. The CEO should not only participate in the hiring of the director of development, but also have the final word on selection.

Development has become more than just raising dollars. The development office usually organizes and is responsible for events, dinners, shows, parties, and a variety of other efforts to reach the public with the organization's message. The development office also coordinates the public relations efforts and the writing, distribution, and dissemination of organizational material, such as newsletters, brochures, and periodic reports to donors. The development office is also responsible for the agency's website and at times other information technology functions.

The CEO, "the face of the organization," is clearly the person whom key stakeholders associate with the not-for-profit. The CEO needs to be the organization's key contact with respect to raising money. The organization's funds usually come from high-net-worth individuals, foundations, corporations, and government. Many not-for-profits receive substantial funds in the form of government grants and contracts. Governmental agencies and their representatives expect to work with the person whom they know best and with whom they have a relationship. Some executives have not understood that securing government resources requires the same intense fundraising skills that are devoted to raising dollars in the private sector. The CEO is the person who best understands the nature of the relationship with the governmental agency, the services to be rendered, the outcomes expected, and the review, evaluation, and audit process built into the specific contract. The CEO is the person held accountable and the main link to the public funds. The same is true for individuals who give substantial donations. Whereas these givers are willing to work with the director of development, most want to have contact with the CEO and trust that he or she is actively engaged in the process of securing and appropriately spending the dollars.

Many foundation heads feel that the content of the request is important but it is the person behind the request and the relationship that the CEO develops with the funding source that determines its success. Agency executives need to understand this fact better than many presently do. They cannot run their organizations well and expect others to raise the money. They can and should receive help from the board, the development director, and others, but they are the principal fundraiser. Organizations that raise substantial amounts of money even during hard times are those who have a strong, trusted, charismatic, and up-front CEO who is able to carry the day and place his or her organization at the top of the donor list.

An executive of a large foundation talked about a meeting she had with the CEO and development director of a major not-for-profit. The CEO was so intent on telling her why he was there, what he wanted from her foundation, and the value of the work that his not-for-profit was doing that he failed to hear what the foundation was interested in funding and what their priorities were. He was not only a poor listener but had failed to read the foundation's published reports and recent requests for proposals (RFPs) and match his proposal with the foundation's interests. He turned off the foundation executive because he sucked the air out of the room and was interested only in a one-way street.

Foundations today want partners and a synergy between the funder and the recipient. Some foundations also try to force a desired project onto the organization's agenda for a specific program or project. A true partnership is one of mutual respect, honesty, and shared goals. Foundations need to understand that it is the not-for-profit service organization that actually executes and implements the program. The service organization can seek advice and counsel from the foundation and must be transparent about its successes and failures. Foundation requests are well received when they reflect careful analysis, use available research data, and are outcome focused. Today, soft, process-oriented requests that have little evidence in support of the proposal are usually filed in a round receptacle. Be direct, forthright, purposeful, and always clear and enthusiastic about your request.

Not-for-Profits, Donors, and Funds

Foundations in 2009 contributed $38.44 billion to not-for-profits (down 8.9% from 2008). The number is staggering. Foundation assets are over $600 billion, with the largest gifts going to universities and religious and cultural institutions, but a substantial and growing amount also goes to service organizations. Many foundations are obligated by law to contribute a minimum of 5 percent of their assets each year to not-for-profit organizations. The key for the CEO is to get to know the heads of foundations, both large and small, especially those whose mission corresponds to that of the not-for-profit. RFPs should be responded to in clear and concise terms that demonstrate what the deliverables will be and the expected outcomes. If an organization is not in a position to know when the RFP will be issued and in what substantive area, then the entire process is academic. Organizations must be on the right list to receive information and applications from government, foundations, and private giving sources.

Larry Kennedy, in *Quality Management in the Nonprofit World* (Reliable Man Books, 2004) states that "an organization that obtains tax exempt status is the beneficiary of a profound opportunity to apply entrepreneurship, compassion and practicality in fulfilling their social responsibility." This statement reflects the importance of not-for-profits delivering on their stated mission in ways that satisfy their tax-exempt status. Receiving dollars from either public or private donors dictates a serious responsibility to deliver on the funds received. Organizations that accept money for a specific purpose and do not apply and use it accordingly risk severe criticism or worse. It is rare, but some organizations have been censured by governmental agencies and in some cases had their tax-exempt status suspended or revoked. Universities have also experienced similar consequences.

Not-for-profits are tax exempt because there is a trade-off between the not-for-profits' work and governmental responsibility to our citizens. In exchange for providing services for the betterment of the community, the not-for-profit is excused from paying taxes and donors to the not-for-profit can deduct that which they contribute from their tax obligation. This arrangement implies a clear relationship between government, donors, and the tax-exempt organization. Not-for-profits need to pay great attention to the way in which they use, apply, or distribute government funds. Some organizations that have affiliates distribute funds to the affiliates, which are often separate not-for-profit corporate structures. When this occurs, the organization that received the funds is accountable and upon audit will be held responsible for how these funds were used. It is important that CEOs and chief financial officers (CFOs) of not-for-profits understand their critical responsibilities in the fiscal area of work. An organization that may be doing great work in the service arena can put itself out of business through fiscal sloppiness or mismanagement. This is an important lesson for organizational leadership.

Recently, many articles have been written about billionaires like Bill Gates and George Soros who have given to organizations that not only have the capacity to provide a needed service but can actually change or transform a dysfunctional system. This is also true for large foundations, including the Goldman-Sachs Foundation, that wish to change large systems such as public schools, health care, nursing homes, housing, and small business creation by leveraging their gifts in ways to secure larger gifts from others or from government. Gates joined with Warren Buffett to address many large-scale needs of poor people both abroad and in the United States in ways that alter housing, health, and education. What does this mean for not-for-profit organizations? Clearly, if agencies are to be players in a significant way they must rethink and adjust their own programs to address these larger issues and secure the funds needed to achieve their new and larger objectives. Often this cannot be done singularly, meaning that not-for-profits need to form collaborations, coalitions, and partnerships, which might also include the funders, to accomplish these system changes over time.

When attracting significantly wealthy donors who share the organization's mission, one must be careful not to rely on a single person or family. Recently, a longtime donor to the American Civil Liberties Union (ACLU) withdrew his annual gift of more than $20 million. That one event punched a 25 percent hole in ACLU's annual operating budget, forcing cutbacks across the board. The donor indicated that market conditions, not any programmatic or philosophical disagreement, caused the discontinuation of funding. The lesson, however, is clear. The ACLU is hoping that its membership will now come to its aid in an attempt to make up for the budget deficit. Sometimes, such a broadening of the donor base, after a funding disaster of this kind, is a blessing in disguise.

Funds Management

The CEO's role with the director of development is similar to the relationship between the CEO and the chief financial officer (CFO). All organizations need a solid, top-flight CFO who is knowledgeable about accounting principles, understands fiscal management, has the proper credentials, and understands the importance of fiscal and fiduciary responsibility. The agency's fiscal position is dependent on sound fiscal management. CEOs need to understand what goes into an operational budget, capital expenditures, restricted funds, endowments, fringe and overhead costs, and board designated and unrestricted funds. These are just some of the categories of budgeting and management the CEO needs to understand and effectively supervise. Small and young organizations, many of which are community based and do extraordinary work with clients, have stumbled with respect to fiscal responsibility. When the numbers are not right and when an organization has trouble accounting for its funds, the work, however highly prized, will not support the organization's continuance. These organizations must recruit knowledgeable accountants or others in the fiscal management area to serve in either a part-time or volunteer capacity until they grow large enough to hire an accomplished CFO. Some organizations have specifically recruited individuals from the business sector to serve on their board and who temporarily serve as fiscal managers. It is essential that all organizations have the proper fiscal and budgetary controls in place so that they do not jeopardize their standing or their existence.

Many executives rely heavily on their CFO and that is appropriate. But such reliance at times allows them to become removed from the process and therefore not educated managers. Clear rules apply to all organizations. There should be periodic fiscal reports, at least quarterly reports to the board or its designated committees, annual independent audits, timely submission of all government reports, and year-end operational and fiscal reports available to the public and where possible on the agency's website.

The CEO should regularly meet with the CFO and be aware of administrative costs relative to the agency's total budget. Overhead costs that exceed 15 to 20 percent in most not-for-profit organizations are considered excessive and can raise serious questions by rating agencies such as CharityNavigator.com and the Better Business Bureau. While agency executives should ensure sound management oversight, supervision, and quality control, the expenditures for these functions should be kept below 25 percent so that 75 cents of every dollar is applied to services. Regular meetings with department heads and those responsible for program implementation should include the CFO to ensure that program and budget expenditures are correlated. Too often, program review is separated from budgetary examination, resulting in great hardship when needed services are reduced or cut because of unplanned overspending.

Budgetary planning is a key function of the CEO and the board, the major fiduciaries of the organization. Budget planning should be a group process and include the key players within the organization. At times it is advisable for the agency's independent auditor also to participate in this process. In projecting budgets for the next fiscal year it is a good idea to underestimate revenue and overestimate expenditures, giving the organization room for making midcourse corrections. The reverse can create serious shortfalls, resulting in hurtful budgetary cuts during the fiscal year. Cash flow is also a major issue, since funding sources from governmental agencies are often not prompt payers. The organization might be able to count on the money, but receipt could be delayed for months or in some instances even up to one year while the organization still needs to pay its employees, taxes, overhead, and programmatic costs on time. Each organization needs to make plans for its cash flow needs so that there will not be a need to borrow at high interest rates or have enormous receivables.

Organizations that receive substantial funding from the government should carefully read the contracts or agreements with that governmental agency. Does the contract cover all costs, including fringes and severance, if warranted, and are there specific cancellation provisions? If tax revenues fall or the economy goes into recession, these grants might be summarily reduced or eliminated. This leaves the not-for-profit in an awkward position and either requires cutting or eliminating the program or finding other funds to continue the service. Some organizations develop their budgets in ways that provide for a rainy-day, contingency, or reserve fund.

The need for a reserve fund or endowment cannot be underestimated. Not-for-profits struggle to raise funds just to cover their yearly budgets and out-of-pocket expenses and many do not think of establishing a restricted fund for future use. That is a mistake. The extent that not-for-profits can use the income generated by endowments that are well invested can make all the difference in program continuation independent of governmental funding. An organization that can count on a certain percentage of income each year from its own endowment has an important element of security, autonomy, and success.

Recently, Rockefeller Philanthropy has been advising foundations on how to adjust their giving in the light of the present economy. It is suggesting a three-year rolling average of the foundations' assets in determining their grant making. Such an approach would reduce the effect of a single year's downturn in the economy and continue to give at the 5 percent annual disbursement level. It also suggests that foundations establish a "bank-like" lending program that will be below market interest rates. Many foundations now understand that they need to help organizations "capacity build," meaning they need to support core operations (management,

administration, and supervision) and not just specific programs to ensure the organizations can survive and provide
sound quality control. These foundations also understand the
need to establish a reserve or endowment fund for agencies
that they support, allowing for longer term financial security.
Some large nonprofits that have, over the years, developed an
endowment have chosen to spend down some of those funds
during times of crisis, such as the recession that we've recently experienced. Those endowment funds carefully apply
to programs that allow for a continuation of services, especially if donations decrease or are used to address a new need.
The New York Times Company Foundation board, upon the
recommendation of its president, voted to spend down some
of its endowment to address the issues of youth unemployment and families at risk of losing their housing during the
subprime era.

Not-for-profits should carefully examine all of the new
opportunities for wealthy donors to give to their organizations. Do not assume they have been advised by their own
financial managers or trust officers about new giving opportunities such as a short-term trust or grantor-retained annuity
trust (GRAT).

Organizations that consciously and systematically diversify
their fundraising base are knowledgeable about changing laws,
regulations, and opportunities for funders and have a clear
statement of purpose and mission.

Summary

- Fundraising is much more sophisticated than in the past
  and combines development, public relations, public information, and website development.

- Development directors should be active members of the management team and report to the executive director or CEO.
- Development directors need to be aware of all new opportunities for raising funds, including deferred-giving programs such as charitable remainder trusts, minitrusts, and a variety of newer tax-saving instruments.
- While boards of trustees have the main responsibility for raising funds, the development director as well as the executive director and other members of the professional staff also have important responsibilities in fundraising.
- Fundraising needs to be actively connected to program services and connected to the organization's strategic direction to be successful.
- The CEO is "the face of the organization" and the key person whom donors and other stakeholders associate with the organization.
- Foundation heads often expect the CEO to be the key professional and available to them. This is also the case with government functionaries.
- Foundation requests should be carefully developed, customized to the specific issue, and data rich where possible.
- Results of funded activities should be transparent and publicized even when the outcomes do not represent complete success.
- Many foundations want to be active partners with the funded organization and be kept involved.
- Organizations should not rely on a single individual or family for a significant part of their agency's budget. Diversification of funding is important.
- The relationship between the CEO, CFO, and the board is one that requires attention with respect to reporting and supervision.

- CEOs should be involved and knowledgeable about the budget-planning process. Budget responsibility should not be left exclusively to the CFO.
- Contracts with government agencies should be carefully reviewed before signing and the organization should be aware of any conflicts or limitations.

Chapter 11

Evaluation, Human Resources, Staff Training, and Development

Evaluation is an essential part of not-for-profit work. In the past, social agencies were able to get by on the basis of reputation, doing community service and "God's work." Today "God's work" must also have data attached. A not-for-profit that cannot show results will have trouble sustaining its operation. If an organization is to be successful and survive, CEOs must be responsible for controlling and monitoring organizational functions and results, which can only be achieved through evaluation research. Accountability, central to the CEO's function, connects the internal work of the organization with external results.

The Evaluation Process

CEOs and managers of not-for-profits have understood their need to run a sound organization, control waste, eliminate fraud, and administer caseloads and programs under their jurisdiction. Managers also need to improve the efficiency and the effectiveness of the organization, which can be done only through a process of review, capacity building, and evaluation of the internal processes needed for effective cost control. Evaluation is central to reviewing which programs are most effective and responsive to the clients' needs, interests, and aspirations. It helps to customize programs to fit the needs of the clients and communities; it is not "one size fits all."

There are any number of different approaches to evaluation—process, outcome, impact—all of which are valid and appropriate. Impact evaluation, of course, is a measure often associated with advocacy efforts and change-oriented efforts. Historically social agencies and their funders have been satisfied by measuring input: how much money is devoted to a particular project. Increasingly, foundations insist on *outcome* measures. Some evaluation is qualitative in nature and often more difficult to justify while other evaluation is quantitative, which allows for a clearer metric. Policy analysis draws heavily on both economic and sociopolitical theory.

Typical questions in evaluation other than the methodologies employed are:

- Did the program achieve its desired outcomes?
- Are the outcomes attributable to the program?
- Is the program the most efficient way to achieve the desired outcomes?
- Has the program met or exceeded preestablished standards?

Process evaluation addresses the following questions:

- Which parts of the program worked well?
- Which parts require improvement?
- Which parts used systematic observation or outside documentation?
- Which aspects of the program underwent quality control review?
- Which internal staff is responsible for program implementation and evaluation?

These questions are typically part of program impact assessment. The CEO and his or her designees should not become invested in the specific issues of methodology, reliability, statistical relevance, and validity. Professionals trained in research design, methodology, and analysis are best able to address these questions. The CEO is well advised to confer with research professionals, and to learn and be briefed on the processes used and understand the work, but does not need to become the expert or the primary principal.

Evaluation usually falls into the following categories:

- *Outcome evaluation*—what were the results?
- *Process evaluation*—the relationship between program implementation and services delivered.

- *Participatory evaluation*—this is not deductive but rather inductive and centered on those who are asking the questions and the respondents.
- *Program self-evaluation*—internal staff reviews their own involvement and process.
- *Cluster evaluation*—bringing together the different groups participating in the process.

Action research has become more frequent during the past decade. The key stakeholders are community activists and those directly affected by the issue at hand. The purpose of this type of evaluation is to achieve change or reduce a social deficit. The methods employed are usually focus groups with stakeholders, key informant interviews, and systematic observation. Typical questions in action research are: What do people in the particular system need? What specific research needs to be done to understand that need or system? What interventions are needed to improve the system? Policymakers often use this form of evaluation to help make alterations in the major system, such as health care, education, employment.

The Theory of Change

Prospective evaluation defines a policy change and projects short- and long-term goals. The effort is to integrate evaluation with program implementation and provide reviewers with indicators of success before large-scale policy change can be achieved. This process is most helpful in delivering feedback, refining strategy, assessing impact, encouraging advocate engagement, and promoting a learning culture. In the *Harvard Family Research Project*, Justin Louie and Kendall Guthrie describe prospective evaluation as being most helpful to legislative and administrative policymakers. They describe a "Theory of Change" that explains how and why a project's activities are expected to lead to desired policy changes. It provides a roadmap based on an assessment of the environment. In some cases, policy change will be one component of a larger social change strategy.

Many organizations are using theory-of-change approaches in their current strategic planning. The process does not have to be overly complicated and can involve a fairly simple set of questions:

- What is the problem you are trying to solve?
- What will be different if you are successful?
- What activities will you undertake to achieve your goal?
- What factors will accelerate or inhibit the process?

Louie and Guthrie suggest that any well-developed theory of change should include specific benchmarks. Often major policy change is a long-term effort and benchmarks are very helpful in establishing milestones along the way.

The CEO, Evaluation, and Human Resources

The CEO needs to create a climate within the organization that promotes evaluation and enlists the right team to conduct program and outcome evaluation. If there is a key message the CEO should impart to staff, it is the following:

- Keep it simple.
- Value capacity building as a key to sound outcome measures.

- Flexibility is a strength, and failure to reach the goal may actually produce important incremental gains.
- Let the story be told; be open and transparent, do not fear community comment, be clear about evaluation expectations, and do not overestimate or overstate what you expect as an outcome.

The CEO is responsible for securing the resources to conduct evaluation. These resources can be internally budgeted or held outside the operational budget, dependent on securing the resources to conduct the study. Intelligent administrators and foundation heads understand that evaluation is not a collateral function, but rather is essential to the effective running of a not-for-profit.

Managing human resources within the not-for-profit is a complicated task. The major resource in not-for-profits is human beings. The CEO is the main manager who establishes the organizational culture, sets the tone, and is the chief purveyor of the values and beliefs of the organization. In medium-size and large not-for-profits, the CEO must employ a human resources (HR) manager or, in highly complex not-for-profits, a team of HR specialists. The HR department is often responsible for aspects of staff training and development, benefits, employment, grievance procedures, supervisory training, and, where necessary, termination arrangements. The HR director or department is part of the administrative and management structure of the organization. Whereas HR functions include opportunities for employee growth and development and are concerned with employee satisfaction, the department nevertheless is a part of management. This fact is very important to identify since employees and at times HR directors become confused as to their primary obligations and responsibilities. The HR director is neither a neutral mediator nor a replacement for a shop steward. HR functions often require degrees of confidentiality, such as referrals to a mental health or alcohol/substance abuse counselor or employee-assistance program (EAP). The HR department is an important entity within the management system of the organization.

HR managers must negotiate issues of efficiency and equity among employees carrying out different job functions, maximize productivity, and develop fair and respectful personnel procedures. HR directors must be aware of and knowledgeable about laws and regulations that govern not-for-profit tax-exempt organizations. The HR department is often responsible for recruitment and selection, compensation and benefits, performance reviews, and plans for retirement. HR participates in creating the procedures and policies that ensure the organization is competitive with other not-for-profits and compliant with all relevant regulations.

Responsibilities of the Human Resources Department

Most not-for-profits today have established EAPs either as a separate internal entity or through a third-party contractual arrangement. This cost-effective arrangement enables employees and members of their families to receive assistance and help. In many cases it allows the employee to continue to be an effective and productive worker and resolves stressful situations. The referral is a protected and confidential process and need not, except in emergencies, be reported to the employee's supervisor or department head. The confidential nature of the procedure must be protected and carefully adhered to.

HR managers have an important collegial and advisory role with respect to department heads and operational managers. HR is often the first stop in matters of employee grievances, workplace safety, and disciplinary actions. HR directors must be in tune with the organization's primary functions and mission and understand that their role is to help sustain productivity and fulfill the agency's service mandate. The HR director should call to the chief executive's attention any issues related to job fairness, hiring practices (particularly with respect to diversity), and concerns regarding possible mismanagement. HR directors must ensure the protection of legitimate whistleblowers and effectively implement any changes brought to their attention. Full compliance with the Civil Rights Act with respect to equality of opportunity is a must for any HR department, which should comply with the letter and spirit of the law.

The HR director should be aware of the Equal Employment Opportunity Act, Equal Pay Act, Pregnancy Discrimination Act, Family and Medical Leave Act, Age Discrimination Act, Americans with Disabilities Act, Fair Labor Standards Act, and, of course, the Social Security Act. Posting job notices both internally and externally is a responsibility of HR, as well as reviewing job applications, developing job descriptions, the initial screening of candidates, and participating in the selection process. The ultimate decision with respect to the hiring of professional employees should be within the province of the CEO or his or her designee and should not exclusively rest with the HR director or department.

The development of a personnel manual, benefits booklet, and listing of compensation arrangements are the responsibility of HR, as well as setting up new staff orientation and training and ongoing staff development programs. On-the-job training and staff development should go beyond orientation and include matters of supervision and coaching where necessary. HR should also be responsible for ensuring employee evaluation, performance reviews, and personnel record keeping.

HR departments need to be especially aware of new developments in the workplace and employment issues. The first is *genetic discrimination*. Advances in genetic testing have enabled employers to use information to penalize prospective or present employees. There have been reports of people being denied jobs or being fired because a parent had a disease such as Huntington's chorea or the gene that predisposes women to breast or ovarian cancer. The Genetic Information Nondiscrimination Act has ushered in a new era. The law prohibits employers from asking for genetic tests or taking into account an employee's genetic background in hiring, firing, or promotion. It prohibits discrimination on the basis of genetic background in group and individual health insurance plans.

Employees who have become pregnant have been protected from discrimination by federal law for some time but many issues still remain. Eilene Zimmerman, in the November 22, 2009 *New York Times*, pointed out that women who have become pregnant while employed often feel left out of important projects and events. Employers are now forced by law to offer maternity leave but the employee may still face negative repercussions in the workplace. HR departments need to be sensitive to the issue. Managers must include pregnant employees in meetings in and out of the office and avoid what Zimmerman calls "benevolent sexism," where women are treated like children who need to be protected.

Staff Training and Development

Staff training and development is an essential component of any progressive and efficient organization. Time should be scheduled and allowances made for staff to participate in ongoing training and development, particularly as it affects their work. Not-for-profits have often assigned more experienced staff to lead training sessions on such topics as relationship building, client outreach, interviewing skills, and culturally relevant practices. Training should not be seen as optional or collateral but necessary for staff to grow, learn new theory, build their knowledge base, and become more effective practitioners. There are times when it is best to make arrangements with a university for more complicated training and for the agency to pay all or part of the costs of tuition for their referred employees. Universities, either through work-study or continuing education programs, are more than happy to make such arrangements and to partner with not-for-profit organizations. Course credit is important for those professionals who wish to advance or be eligible for new roles or promotion. Organizations that provide ongoing internal or university-based staff development programs tend to have much lower turnover rates and enjoy a higher ratio of productivity than those that do not.

Organizations often tend to reduce or eliminate staff training and development when budgets get tight and balance sheets are tenuous. While budget modifications are often necessary, executives should not think first of reducing professional training and development. In some instances it is the very last thing that should be cut.

In an article in the *Harvard Mental Health Newsletter* (No. 4, November 2008), "Dealing with the Emotional Aspect of

Conflict," Dr. Daniel Shapiro, director of the Harvard International Negotiation Initiative, provides some very helpful information to not-for-profit executives, particularly HR directors. He identifies appreciation, encompassing the desire to be valued and understood, as a key in preventing employee conflict and helping to resolve disputes. Shapiro believes affiliation, a "we" and "us" feeling among staff, is important. Building a team, creating a sense of community and respect for colleagues' autonomy, status, and role are key elements in staff training and resolving staff conflicts.

HR functions obviously involve a great many interlocking steps and strategies to help the organization achieve its goals through an effective and stable workforce. HR is an important conduit between management and employees that ensures that the agency's mission is understood and service obligations fulfilled.

Summary

- Evaluation is an essential part of all organizations.
- Evaluation is helpful in establishing a sound organization, controlling waste, eliminating fraud, and defining program jurisdictions.
- Evaluation can come in many forms: process, outcome, and impact. Evaluation can be qualitative and/or quantitative in nature and allow for the development of a clear metric for analysis.
- Evaluation should not be seen as either extra work or a burden but rather as an active part of the organization's management system.
- Evaluation and its outcomes are key in soliciting government funding.

- The "Theory of Change" is part of the organization's roadmap, which is used as the backdrop to evaluating program impact.
- Resources to support evaluation are hard to come by and at times the organization needs to rely on board donations or unrestricted funds to support that activity.
- All organizations need to be aware of managing human resources and where possible have a human resources director or department.
- Human resources staff should be responsible, in large measure, for developing personnel practice manuals, conflict-of-interest reports, and codes of conduct. HR should also be responsible for staff development training and employee-assistance programs.
- The human resources director is an important and vital part of the management system of the agency.
- The HR director should be included in most administrative and programmatic meetings so that he or she can become thoroughly familiar with all aspects of the organization's work.
- The HR director should be the most knowledgeable person with respect to the Equal Employment Opportunity Act, Pregnancy Prevention Discrimination Act, Family and Medical Leave Act, Americans with Disabilities Act, and other acts, legislation, and regulations.
- The HR department should be also the first place available to employees who have a grievance or are legitimate whistleblowers.
- When budgets are tight, research and development and human resources are often the first programs to be cut or eliminated. That's a big mistake.

Chapter 12

The Age of Technology

At no time in our history has technology been more central to our lives. Technology and its management extend far beyond microchips, iPods, cell phones, MySpace, Facebook, Twitter, and whatever comes next. The successful integration of information technology (IT) into the human services organization depends heavily on the knowledge and sensitivity of the CEO and his or her appointees. Effective use of technology can be an incredible tool in providing better services to the community.

The Importance of Technology

We now take e-mail for granted, and although it can be overused and depersonalized it is clearly here to stay. Professional journals, newspapers, magazines, and almost all publications are available on the Internet. Every quote in the stock market and every baseball score can be secured in real time. For social agencies, the opportunity to download vast amounts of information to assist us in our work, particularly in effective budgetary and case management, is striking. Confidential material can be stored electronically, thereby eliminating handwritten notes and index cards. We can now use computer systems for enforcement of child support, quality control of food stamp distribution, computer-assisted continuing education programs, and client intake and diagnostic work. Clearly, those social work managers who resist IT advances are seen as dinosaurs.

Social agencies facing budgetary shortfalls want to preserve their resources for client services and, understandably, at times resist spending hard-earned dollars on upgrading technology systems. Technology is expensive; during the past 10 years, every administrator has learned to build in a budget item for it and not view it as a one-time expense. Capacity building is dependent on our ability to manage technology in what is sometimes referred to as "paperless" staff activity. IT should be introduced in stages and with training so that staff can keep pace with those changes. Without training, insecurity and demoralization will surely set in.

The mission of the organization and the vision of its leadership should be the driving forces in the organization, with technology offering greater opportunities to achieve sound results. The skill of the executive in hiring IT people is no less important than in hiring skilled clinicians or policy analysts.

The IT people need to understand that they are working for a social agency and must accept the goals, objectives, and practices of the organization. The technology staff must be integrated within the professional system of the organization so they are not isolated so as to constitute a fifth column.

It is essential that managers under the leadership of the CEO help all staff understand the inevitability of change within human services organizations. With training and time, staff will not be overwhelmed by the introduction of new technology or feel threatened by their inability to master it and fear loss of employment. The following are steps that are important for managers to implement. Some of these guidelines are referenced in *The Social Worker as Manager* (5th ed.), by Robert W. Weinbach:

- Provide assurances and continuity: New technology will not change the focus on client services but rather enhance our ability to more effectively serve our clients.
- Wherever possible, use existing staff as trainers; this will help to provide a continued sense of belonging and mutual support.
- Ensure that the use of new technology does not preclude face-to-face client contact and personal interaction.
- Reassure clients that confidential data stored in the computer will be protected.
- Make sure the mission of the organization drives the need for technology and its important uses, not the other way around.
- Know when to say "no" to any technology change that might violate client confidentiality and overwhelm staff.

Experts in this area of work have identified a number of important functions that should be integrated into our work. The protection of data (encryption) is most important, especially in relation to Health Insurance Portability and Accountability Act (HIPAA) policy. Information to assist social workers who are required to abide by client privacy policies is also found under the Health Information Technology for Economic and Clinical Health (HITECH) Act. Both of these acts have been clarified, now requiring notification to clients if there is an unauthorized release of private health records, specifically if the information is not encrypted. The utilization of groupware such as Microsoft Exchange is most important to facilitate interoffice communication and shared contacts and files. Obviously, confidentiality of the material must be maintained at all times.

It is recommended that all organizations periodically review their database architecture to assure contemporary usage. This can be accomplished through outsourcing and is usually the least expensive way to achieve this end. Those organizations that consider themselves too small to hire an IT staff member can either hire an offsite consultant on a modest retainer or train a present staff person to become the in-house "techie."

External communication is most easily accomplished through use of Google modules and similar programs.

Most executives presently understand that budgetary purchasing and human resources data can be provided and stored online, as well as performance reviews and evaluation.

Several large for-profit enterprises, such as Accenture and Oracle, have jointly developed technology solutions for social services agencies. They have created integrated software packages to address the needs of social services agencies in such areas as case management and outcome focus program delivery.

With respect to fundraising, online donations have become an amazing source of revenue. During the past nine years, donations collected through the New York Times Neediest Cases Fund have gone from 5 to 42 percent. Not-for-profits who have updated and active websites should pay attention to this to ensure that donors have an easy way to make contributions. This is especially true for younger supporters, who are very technology savvy.

Digital management can be an important way to open traditional top-down managerial processes and engage the staff and colleagues to participate from the start. The shorthand term is *crowd sourcing*—soliciting the wisdom of the group in response to problems both big and small. This same digital management approach can also be an opportunity for clients to participate in the process of suggesting remedies on issues and problems. The general public can now also participate through Facebook and Twitter and whatever comes next in the work in the not-for-profit.

A Web presence is clearly of great importance; a site that is updated, looks good, and makes sense aesthetically is a most valuable tool for social agencies. There are many firms and individuals who can help establish this kind of attractive website.

Technology and its proper use can be a most effective tool in improving the organization's services, attracting better-trained staff, and reducing the need for time-consuming and unproductive paperwork. If used correctly, the technology can reduce staff turnover and burnout. The key is effective preparation and training of all staff within the organization.

Summary

- Effective use of technology is an important tool to provide an efficient service.

- All organizations need to develop electronic systems to enhance their work as well as an active website to inform employees, donors, and the public at large of the organization's work.
- Budget planning should annually include a line item for IT.
- Capacity building is somewhat dependent on the organization's ability to manage technology and free staff from their paper burden.
- IT personnel are no less important than skilled clinicians and practitioners and should be integrated into the agency's structure and employment system.
- All professional staff should become proficient in the use of technology; where possible, the agency should become "paperless."
- Be knowledgeable of the HIPAA and HITECH Act requirements.
- Use technology to grow fundraising.
- Use digital management to open up staff, client, and public communication and input.

Chapter 13

Volunteers and Voluntarism

The need for volunteers today is as great as ever. Our not-for-profit sector is battling severe financial constraints while facing growing demands to provide services for those in need. The twenty-first century marks the emergence of growing institutionalized forms of volunteer activity. Volunteers throughout the world, from all walks of life and of all ages, are facing new challenges to improve lives. Broad participation of volunteers is furthering health and human services, arts and culture, education, environmental protection, and civic development.

The Growth of Voluntarism

Volunteers have been marshaled to address the consequences of calamitous disasters such as earthquakes, tsunamis, and epidemics. It is estimated by the independent sector that 44 percent of all adults serve as volunteers, which represents over 80 million people or the equivalent of 9 million full-time employees at a dollar value of just under $240 billion. Museums, day care, Little League, concerts, public parks, voluntary clinics, hospitals, homes for senior citizens, Meals on Wheels, and shelters for the homeless all exist because of voluntarism. An example of the growth can be seen in public high schools and charter schools throughout our country, where voluntarism has grown from 27 percent to 83 percent since 1984. This growth was fueled by *service learning,* where public and charter schools have students engaged in community work as part of their curriculum. College admission criteria often include a service learning component that values what it takes to make a good life, not merely a good living. Once in college or graduate school, students are often required to take courses in voluntarism, not-for-profit work, and, at the graduate level, management and governance in not-for-profit organizations. When students graduate they provide a powerful force in contributing their knowledge and passion, which strengthens the not-for-profit sector. Organizations such as Teach for America, AmeriCorps, and City Year were all founded and grew through the voluntary efforts of their leaders and board members.

Stephanie Strom said in her December 29, 2009 *New York Times* article, "Does Service Learning Really Help?," that while service learning, defined as community service, supplements and enhances what students learn in the classroom, all is not positive. Some service learning volunteers, she reports, have indicated that their not-for-profits were not organized administratively to effectively train and supervise them. Though some organizations pay a coordinator to direct the volunteers, others shortcut the process, trying to save expenses, and assign the task to a professional who may already be overburdened. She states, "If service learning is not well coordinated by the academic institution it can place a heavy burden on the community partner," and parenthetically, the service learner.

Volunteers are found in almost all programs serving senior citizens, from food service to home visits for the medically indigent. Corporate voluntarism has also made a significant mark on our service landscape. Many corporations expect their employees to volunteer, and in some instances provide work-release time. Some volunteer programs are seasonal or holiday driven while others are on a more continuous basis, such as weekly tutoring, mentoring children, or serving food to the homeless. Some volunteer programs, such as Habitat for Humanity, require group activity that may last several weeks while constructing housing units, ball fields, and public parks.

Many volunteers are engaged in fundraising, sponsoring donor lunches and dinners, and honoring community leaders or heroes. Some volunteers provide management assistance, and others provide Young Leaders Training Programs so that emerging leaders can assume positions in not-for-profits in the not-too-distant future. In general, volunteers constitute an important workforce that expands the capacity for not-for-profits to address the increasing demands placed upon them.

Relationship between Volunteers and Management

While volunteering is an important part of American life, organizational leaders must recognize that volunteer services are not free. For organizations to effectively place and use volunteers they must understand that a financial investment is needed to yield desirable outcomes. All volunteers need structure, guidance, direction, and a sense of belonging. Without attention provided by the CEO and the professional staff, volunteers can become discouraged and feel unwanted and unsure of their place within the organization. Such dissatisfaction can contribute to their dropping out and looking for something more promising. Not-for-profits need to invest time in recruiting, but also in providing sound volunteer organization and ongoing training. The best way to discourage volunteers who come with hearts full of goodwill is to not provide the structure, time, and attention that they need to galvanize their energy and productivity. A structured volunteer program requires a permanent staff position to ensure that the programs are running well and that volunteers have a point of contact. Usually each dollar invested in a professional volunteer trainer can yield multiple dollars of volunteer time.

Top-level support, starting with the CEO, must recognize the worth of the investment and extol the value of volunteering throughout the organization. The CEO must provide a proper budget for that service and ensure that policies are developed with respect to volunteer training. Prior to the acceptance of a volunteer, child abuse and criminal background checks and medical screening should be completed for those who might have contact with clients. Prospective volunteers should be interviewed at least once and demonstrate their willingness to participate in an ongoing training program. Internal arrangements for the reimbursement of snacks or lunches and transportation or trip costs should be implemented rapidly without there being a discouraging bureaucratic process. Some organizations historically have had too narrow a view of the people who should constitute the volunteer force. There are times when volunteers can also be recipients of services—senior citizens, youth, or board members who wish to have a hands-on experience. All should be welcome.

It is always a good idea for the volunteer to get to know the CEO and other top management staff and for there to be volunteer-recognition events at least once a year if not more often. Volunteers might be invited to the agency's Christmas party or similar event to help them feel part of the organization.

In a *New York Times* article (November 22, 2009), Ariel Kaminer writes, "Thanksgiving is to hunger groups what Halloween is to a costume company." Joel Berg, executive director of the Coalition Against Hunger, said that there are so many volunteers who want to serve food on Thanksgiving that sometimes organizations have to make work for them. Helping people to apply for food stamps will do a lot more to end hunger than serving for two hours on Thanksgiving or Christmas Day. Organizations can help volunteers understand that they can provide important sustained help by making a longer and larger commitment than spending two hours on one day. Some volunteers, based on their own background, can serve as wonderful advocates for the program or mission of the organization. A well-established and highly esteemed individual delivering specific testimony before the city council or local government agency can serve a more potent function than the CEO.

CEOs also need to understand that their primary volunteer group is the board of directors. Boards are made up of volunteers and even though it is a powerful arm of the not-for-profit they are nevertheless a volunteer group. Board members carry considerable power and authority and as individual members require the same attention as any other volunteer group. They need to know they are respected and wanted, have a clear role and function, and enjoy a relationship with key professionals within the organization. CEOs need to see themselves as the board's group worker, organizer, and practitioner. They need to consciously work with the board in building cohesion, creating loyalty to the organization, and developing shared values that enable the board to be organizationally effective. The board, like all other groups, has a defined role and status. Certain board members, quite aside from their designated official roles (Chairperson, President, or Nominating Committee Chairperson), become identified by their fellow board members as clarifier, contrarian, dissident, compromiser, or decision maker. CEOs also need to understand each board member's unique role in the group so they can constructively influence the group dynamic. They need to see their role with the board as central to the group's functioning but not at the center of the group's life. They need to encourage participation and distribute authority and power to help the board and its members have an enlarged vision of participation. Effective work with the board requires the CEO to spend considerable time working with, thinking about, and actively engaging in the process of board development. Effective boards require effective CEO leadership and ineffective boards usually translate into an ineffective CEO. CEOs must use their leadership position in working with volunteer funders, donors, advisory councils, governmental agencies, and local boards.

While volunteers usually come to the organization because they want to be of service to others, many are also volunteering as a way to secure a paid job, enlarge their friendship network, meet people, and spend quality time. These diverse interests are acceptable, but need to be molded so that volunteers find common cause. Volunteers who have an ulterior motive and want to use their position to secure a business vendorship or contract or have an extreme personal need should be counseled out. This is a delicate process that illustrates the need for a professional to be the key contact person for volunteer programs.

Volunteers play a major role in organizational life. They are never, however, a replacement for the professional. Good volunteer programs require solid professional input and clear delegation of responsibilities. If done right, volunteers can constitute an important and powerful component of an agency's functioning and influence. An example of a wonderful volunteer-oriented program is ReServe, which pays a modest stipend of $10 an hour for 15 hours a week for each volunteer. The small stipend essentially creates a contract between the organization and the volunteer, which adds both status and responsibility to the volunteer's role.

Summary

- In difficult economic times, volunteers are often a way of continuing the organization's services.
- The independent sector indicates that 44 percent of all adults volunteer in some way or another.
- Volunteers come from all walks of life—senior citizens, high school students, or church/social/fraternal club members.
- Service learning has become a major source of school-based volunteer activities, as well as corporate voluntarism where employees are provided with work-release time to work for not-for-profit organizations.
- Volunteers can be engaged in fundraising as well as service projects and help with administrative functions.

- Volunteers need structure, guidance, and direction, and need to be part of the organization's system.
- Large organizations may need to establish a volunteer department to ensure ongoing training, supervision, and monitoring of volunteers.
- Board members are also volunteers and need to be seen in that light by the executive director and professional staff.
- Volunteers should not be given "busy work" but assigned to legitimate functions and outcomes that benefit the organization.
- Volunteers can also serve as a recruiting system to enlarge the organization's donor base and in some cases be a training ground for board membership.

Chapter 14

International Social Welfare and the Role of the University

T he world as we know it has shrunk. What takes place on Wall Street is felt not only in Paris and London but also in Timbuktu. The geography may be the same, but the demographics are not. Countries that were once homogeneous with stable populations and eighth- or ninth–generation lineage have largely become polyglots and quite heterogeneous. Population shifts since World War II, and especially in the past decade, have been meteoric. Much of this change is due to ever-increasing mobility, searching for jobs, a common language, greater political and economic freedom, and accessibility. Some of the changes, however, were due to catastrophic events, as with Uganda, Darfur, Bosnia, Kosovo, Croatia, and scores of other upheavals.

France, especially in Paris and other big cities, now has large Algerian, Tunisian, Moroccan, and West African populations. The Netherlands, once totally homogeneous, now has a major influx of Bosnians, Croatians, and other Muslim constituents. Telecommunications, stealth technology, and satellite observation have made the world more visible and smaller. The economic and social systems have all had to change and, interestingly, the social problems faced in many countries throughout the world are very similar. Homelessness, domestic violence, child abandonment and abuse, and sex trafficking are common problems in almost every country. The economic downturn caused enormous unemployment, family breakup, and general insecurity, and has created a social tsunami. The international community was forced to respond to this crisis in ways it had resisted in the past. Economic and social programs were integrated across national boundaries to fix fractured economies and restore stability.

Not-for-Profits' Increasing International Presence

The U.S. government, for example, invested more dollars in AIDS prevention and treatment in Africa beginning in the year 2000 than all of its aggregated funds earmarked for that region for the prior 10 years. The International Monetary Fund and agencies of the United Nations contributed both money and resources to combat diseases that threatened the entire world. Natural disasters and pandemics, including the recent "swine flu" scare, have also created an international response—everything from airport inspections to mass immunizations. The private sector, such as the Gates or Buffett Foundations, as well as older non-governmental organization (NGO) investments, such as the Ford and Rockefeller Foundations, have poured billions of dollars into the effort to combat starvation and hunger and treat AIDS, malaria, tuberculosis, and other diseases.

These efforts required not only money and mission but also personnel. Where did the staff-power come from? Some was generated indigenously and in some parts of the world extensive training was developed to deal internally with what was seen as a needed sovereign response. In most countries, however, trained doctors, mental health specialists, public health practitioners, social workers, and environmentalists needed to be imported. The United States enlarged its Peace Corps activities substantially. Catholic Relief Organizations sprang into action. Newer organizations such as Doctors Without Borders and International Children's Services stepped up their level of activity. People of goodwill joined in the effort by contributing dollars and where possible raising the level of awareness. The United States, with its advanced university system, history of philanthropy, and plethora of social services and NGOs, was in the best position to provide assistance. Schools of social work, education, and psychology not only offered courses and graduate programs in International Social Welfare, but in many cases set up both student and faculty exchanges. Common ground was forged with input from both university faculty and those in charge of governmental or foundation programs in countries in need of assistance.

While some programs dealt with attachment issues, loss, and bereavement (e.g., in Bosnia and Darfur), other modalities were thought to be of even greater relevance. In many instances, programs dealing with causes rather than consequences or conditions were needed. Major programs in immunization, water purification, land reform, farming techniques, and elimination of land mines were all part of the social policy framework. Social workers and other professionals, aside from their clinical practice skills, needed once again to see themselves as reformers, if not revolutionaries. Within existing cultures, programs of change needed to be initiated, affecting not merely habits and family patterns but behaviors. We see this with respect to reproductive health, child support, protection of minors, and respect for women.

Social work was in many ways returning to its earlier roots, not only in helping the individual better adjust to society, but in reshaping society's laws and values and providing assistance to better serve its citizens. An activist international effort was underway, without imperialism and colonialism, but rather with a deep and ongoing respect for the people, their culture, and their aspirations.

Universities' Expanding Involvement

Universities played a significant role in this effort. Teacher training programs became a centerpiece along with language development and training to assure that sufficient numbers of teachers would be available for export. Incidentally, the U.S. Department of Education is also concerned with the retraining of teachers to effectively instruct U.S. students, especially those who are poor and have been alienated from the educational experience.

Universities partnered with important innovators such as Wendy Kopp, Allen Khazei, and Eric Schwarts in developing outstanding programs such as Teach for America, City Year, and a variety of other teaching fellows programs. These programs were applicable for training teachers for schools in the United States and for students abroad.

Universities and colleges have also been keenly aware of their responsibility to provide greater accessibility and opportunity for America's school children. American students drop out of high school at an average rate of 1 every 26 seconds. In large urban districts, only half of the students graduate from high school, and of those that do, only a third are ready to move on to four-year colleges. The ethnic groups with the worst outcomes in public school achievement are African Americans and Latinos. The achievement gap between these groups and their Caucasian and Asian American peers is already apparent in kindergarten and continues to grow. Universities have begun to use their expertise and leadership to correct this enormous inequity.

University-based programs, particularly those that reach out to the neighborhood where they are located, need to involve leaders, consumers, and potential students on a variety of important advisory boards and committees. All too often, colleges and universities are removed and in some instances alienated from the communities that surround them. Such outreach is particularly important where ethnic, racial, and cultural diversity concerns are major and ongoing issues that affect the university's relationship with community leaders and residents. Many universities have learned the hard way that they need to spend both time and dollars cultivating sound relationships with community people. Developing programs under university auspices or in partnership with community organizations is a sound way of creating a common agenda.

The Harvard Graduate School of Education is creating a new doctoral degree to focus on leadership in education. The three-year program, tuition-free and conducted in collaboration with the Harvard Business School and Kennedy School of Government, is poised to create dynamic new leaders who will offer creativity, intellectual rigor, and the professionalism needed to help transform public education in the United States. The Harvard program, while just a beginning, attempts to reconcile the need for educational reform with an understanding of sound management and educational advocacy. Educational leaders must understand pedagogy but also management, accountability, and the psychosocial needs of students.

U.S. Secretary of Education Arne Duncan recently said that we are competing with countries that have a ministry of education bringing good ideas to scale. We are challenged to do the same.

Joanie Lipman, in her October 24, 2009, *New York Times* article, "The Mismeasure of Woman," described a striking imbalance of women in the workforce. The gains, Lipman points out, are that "we now have a female Speaker of the House and Secretary of State, and thirty-two women have served as governors, and thirty-eight as senators." The news is not so wonderful when we look at women in leadership and management roles in science and CEOs in major American companies. In the United States, women earn $0.77 for every dollar a man earns. But more to the point, there are only 15 women who are CEOs in Fortune 500 companies. As serious as the case is for women in the United States, the situation is far worse for women abroad, especially in third-world countries. Women are still treated as indentured servants and in some cases as sex slaves. This is true not only in countries such as Haiti and many in West Africa, but also in a number of Eastern European countries.

If universities are to use their position as enlightened crucibles for change and equality, they must also present that face to the larger community, especially where universities establish satellite locations around the world. New York University, for example, has just established a teaching relationship with the government of Abu Dhabi. This relationship and combined academic facilities can do much to improve conditions in Abu Dhabi, especially if the university offers the opportunity for female students and teachers to have equal rights along with their male counterparts. This can represent a strong political statement that the university is serious about its commitment to freedom, equality, self-determination, and the rights of all, regardless of gender, to a full and free life. The same is true with respect to the influence that university faculty can have in that country with respect to the rights of gay and lesbian students and those of non-Muslim faith. Respecting one's culture and history, while very important, does not mean that collaborations should not also advance the ideals that are the inalienable rights of all people.

United Nations Secretary-General Ban Ki-moon reported in a *New York Times* article (September 18, 2009) that the working poor are suffering throughout the world. He indicated, "there is talk of green shoots of recovery, but our data show another picture. It is not the chronic poor who are most affected, but the near and working poor, whose lives (prior to the economic downturn) improved significantly over the last decade . . . and are now suffering again." As many as 222 million workers run the risk of joining the ranks of the poor, earning less than $1.25 a day, according to the International Labor Organization. Hunger rates are up in every region of the world and 50 million people are now living in extreme poverty. These are the facts and they add up to the need for a massive effort to confront these issues realistically and to win the battle for survival.

American social welfare and universities have a rare if not compelling opportunity to use their strength, knowledge, wealth, and human capital to address these issues both here and overseas. Governments can and must do much but the private sector and our ever-growing not-for-profit universe must also step into the breach in even more significant ways to address the catastrophic events around the world. If we have the political will and the capacity to change, we can make an enormous difference as we did after World War II in reconstructing Europe through the Marshall Plan, revitalizing Japan, and our Point Four Program for Greece and Turkey. The help that we can provide around the world will of course most benefit the people abroad, but let us not forget that ever-increasing numbers in the United States have left their countries to escape famine, hunger, disease, and unemployment by coming to the United States either legally or otherwise. In New York, the largest growing segment of our population is now made up of Mexicans, Dominicans, others from Central and South America, and Southeast Asians. Assisting these countries also provides an enormous service to those nationals living in our country and provides the best and most progressive deterrent to those who immigrate to our shores but would rather stay in their own countries if greater opportunity existed.

Bill George, professor of Management Practice at Harvard Business School, has written:

> Optimistic, forward-thinking leaders are sitting on a rare opportunity, and they must be systematic in how they take advantage of it if they want to make positive changes. Leaders must be willing to ask for help. They should rely on a mentor, an internal management team and an external support group. No one can be an effective leader in a crisis

by attempting to go it alone. Leaders must be the first to recognize this reality and plan accordingly.

Summary

- Social problems have become similar throughout the world; homogeneous countries have become heterogeneous with the influx of large immigrant populations.
- Social work and non-government organizations are playing a larger role in helping countries face perplexing social problems.
- Major foundations such as Gates and Buffett are playing a significant role in issues such as world hunger, HIV/AIDS, homelessness, tuberculosis, and malaria.
- Universities and graduate schools are paying more attention to international work and opportunities.
- Social work, with its orientation to systems change and reform, is in a unique position to be helpful.
- Universities that have study programs abroad are also in a favorable position to provide internships and teaching opportunities in foreign countries.
- Universities such as Harvard and Columbia are now combining programs in education, social work, and public health in an effort to become interdisciplinary.
- Universities can play a major role in redressing the issues of the imbalance of women's rights and workforce inequality.
- Inequality of treatment of women in the United States requires attention and should be addressed by universities and professional associations.

Chapter 15

Succession and Retirement

S uccession, if not planned carefully and in a timely manner, can lead all enterprises on a path to decline. Succession is hard to plan for since often there are many psychological barriers to overcome. Organizations or boards have at times been left leaderless because of death or disability without a succession plan. Strong organizations and executives know that a succession plan must be in place, even when it involves the planning for one's own replacement.

Often, leaders do not adequately prepare for succession, or believe that they are preparing for succession but in reality plan for their own continuation. While some leaders are ready to step down, many think that they can go on indefinitely. Leaders often have a view of themselves as not just central to the organization but indispensable. They justify their decision to stay at the top not to remain in power but rather as their obligation to the enterprise for fear it would tumble in their absence.

Leaders in the not-for-profit arena are no different from their counterparts in the for-profit world. Planning your own professional departure with its attendant loss of status, prestige, and power is difficult, and for some, impossible. Explanations always exist as to why one should stay a little longer, which becomes much longer, which at times becomes indefinite. (The graveyard is full of indispensables.)

Who I Was and Who I Am Now

Interestingly, when the issue of postretirement is discussed among retirees they often define themselves in terms of "who I was" rather than "who I am." This is a sad commentary and reflection of how we perceive ourselves and believe others perceive us with respect to the occupational roles that once defined us. Too often succession is left to another day, or, as one board member said, "We'll get to it in due time." Many organizations are content with their current leadership and would rather not contemplate the difficult and emotional issues attached to succession. Boards are resistant to spending the time and money needed to engage in a proper process of selection—the establishment of a search committee—and wish to avoid the anxiety that accompanies change. Promoting from within or searching outside of the organization also creates tension. Do we hire a search firm? Do we survey the field ourselves? Do we include our present CEO in the process? How confidential should the process be? What happens if there's a leak and it causes embarrassment? Should we consider the second in command and does he or she possess the qualities needed to become number one?

There is always some fear in bringing in a new person, particularly one of great experience and status who might want to radically change the nature and culture of the organization. People give lip service to change, but the status quo is often more comfortable. The current CEO should have a key role, not necessarily in the process of selection of his or her successor but in educating the board and helping them to understand the process and become less anxious and fearful about the end result. The current CEO should help the board better understand the network of services that exist and might even suggest candidates who would be a good fit. The CEO also needs to empower the board or the board's search committee to move forward, to not allow inertia to overcome the driving force, and to not feel that they are abandoning the current CEO as they select a replacement.

The Effects of Retirement on the CEO

The idea of retirement for most CEOs is confusing at best. While some welcome the notion of less stress and anxiety and an easier and more relaxing lifestyle, many do not prepare adequately. Retirement begs the questions: What are you going to do with your newfound time? What hobbies or avocations do you have? Does the golf course await you? Is more leisurely travel in your plans? Will you spend more time with your children or grandchildren? These are real and pertinent questions but they are all external and deal only with concerns of activity and the consumption of time. The answers to these questions identify activities that are essentially substitutions for what was the drive, energy, and challenges that are at the heart of the life of an active CEO.

The emotional or internal issues should be addressed by the retiree and his family before he steps down. Retirement affects one's sense of self, reduces status, often greatly reduces income, and sometimes diminishes self-esteem. It comes back to the "who I was" phenomenon. The retiree no longer has the same connection, admiration, and affection that she once enjoyed from her board and staff. Once retired, she no longer has power and influence and, like it or not, people quickly shift their allegiances and loyalties to her replacement. That is a hard blow and, even if anticipated, not easily absorbed emotionally. All retirees who are in executive positions face this to one degree or another. This is particularly true for those executives who remain within the organization as a consultant, special advisor, or in emeriti status. Executives have said that they felt a difference the very first day that they came to the office after they no longer enjoyed the title of "the boss." Some have said that even the greetings and feeling tone from staff were different and while former subordinates were courteous and respectful there was a noticeable change in the way in which they were approached. Some executives said that they felt unwanted and in the way or were in competition with their replacement. Several felt they were no longer loved by the people who previously offered emotional support. That is hard for anyone in that position, regardless of his emotional strength and strong sense of self. It's a major change. To the extent that one prepares for it, it can be either an emotional setback or understood as part of the process of change.

Much has been written on the need for CEOs to take care of themselves. Many are so consumed with the job at hand that they neglect good health practices such as having regular meals, getting enough sleep, and engaging in cultural and recreational activities. Many complain that they are spending insufficient time with their families and by the time they realize it their children are grown and everyone has missed the rewards of family life. It has been suggested that CEOs who have made the effort within their very busy schedule to relax, take some time off, attend their children's concerts and ball games, and join their family on annual vacations are better able emotionally to adjust to the new lifestyle after they step down. The extent to which executives are aware of their needs and limitations during their working years is a barometer of how they will adjust to a new lifestyle. Being able to share feelings, have an active friendship or peer group, and become a part of communal life is important to adjusting to the next stage. The relationship between the CEO who stepped down and his successor is also a matter of concern. Those who have experienced this process would most likely say to wait patiently for your successor to come to you with questions or seeking advice. Don't presume to know that your advice and ideas will be solicited or accepted easily. Let the relationship develop and play itself out. The relationship is as delicate as an early marriage; people need to get accustomed to their new relationship, roles, and responsibilities.

One high-level executive recently said, "I awakened the morning after my official retirement and felt different, less important, less powerful, and less myself"—an interesting comment, and one that many executive retirees never prepare for or anticipate. As a culture and as a society we seldom engage, at least at the executive level, in an analysis of the psychology of change. What will it do to my psyche and how will it affect my standing and status?

Many executives contemplating retirement will do well to find either a self-help or collegial mutual-aid group and engage and discuss these issues prior to stepping down. Doing so will often provide them with an understanding of their own psychological makeup and reduce pain. A colleague recently said, "I used to work sixty or seventy hours a week, seldom was able to have weekday dinners with my family, and was out of the house most of the time. After retirement, when my schedule was greatly altered, my wife said to me after a few weeks, 'Why are you moping around? Don't you have something to do, and do you realize how many adjustments we have had to make to accommodate your new schedule?'" One's retirement affects the entire family and is in a sense a family issue. It is a sound process for family members to engage with the prospective retiree on an examination of the issues that will affect them, their routines, and family lifestyle.

In the October 15, 2009 issue of the *New York Times* Special Section on Retirement, all of the articles with the exception of one dealt with externals: How will the stock market and current home values affect your means to retire? What kind of IRA is best for you? Does your 401(k) plan allow you to step down? What is the state of your savings? One article talked about ways to ease the pressure of a cash crunch. Another article actually dealt with finding another job through online networking. The only article in the entire supplement that remotely dealt with the psychological aspect of retirement was one that offered the opportunity for retirees to give back through service projects such as teaching or volunteering in schools. The *New York Times*'s supplement clearly reflects the present anxiety in our economy and its effect on retirement, but also once again concentrates on the external factors exclusively with little attention given to the psychosocial.

Succession Planning

There are a number of things that Jim Collins suggests in both *Good to Great* (HarperCollins, 2005) and *How the Mighty Fall* (HarperCollins, 2009) that should be especially avoided by boards of directors:

- Do not rely on a dominating leader who fails to develop strong successors, drives away those who show strength, and thereby creates a leadership vacuum when he or she finally steps away.
- When the CEO departs or dies unexpectedly, no strong replacement is able to step smoothly into the role. This suggests that succession planning needs to begin early, long before the board or the CEO anticipates stepping down.
- Carefully note when strong successor candidates turn down the opportunity to be the CEO. Something obviously is not right within the organization if that occurs with some frequency.
- The board of directors is divided on the designation of a leader, which creates an adversarial dynamic at the top.
- CEOs who continually find reasons for staying on long after they announced that they will be leaving.
- Bringing in successors who do not fit the values, mission, and culture of the organization.
- Something is definitely awry when the board chronically fails at getting the right CEO for the position.

These are some guidelines that would be helpful to the board and search committee:

- A leader who appreciates the role of the board, and is a team player, a self-starter, and anything but a follower.
- A successor who will build on the strengths of her predecessor, but not one who cannot also see the weaknesses that she may be inheriting.
- A leader who is prepared to stay for a sufficient period of time to ensure continuity and continuation of the agency's important service mission. Agencies can endure only so many transitions in a short period of time.

Boards also need to help their new executive have realistic expectations and not feel that they must surpass the leader they are replacing. The best leaders are those who recognize the need to build an executive team and craft a culture that does not depend on a single heroic leader. Whereas no leader can single-handedly build an enduring great organization, the wrong leader can almost single-handedly bring an organization down. Basic reference checking goes without saying, but the informal network is the best source of information about a potential candidate. Defensive practices with respect to forthright references at times make it difficult to get a true picture of a candidate, but knowing informal sources who have previously worked with or supervised him can give a much more accurate, off-the-record assessment. Most importantly, selecting the person who will be instrumental to the effective running of the organization is a process that should not be short-changed. The board search committee should take its time evaluating each candidate, narrow down the applicants to the best three, and carefully debate the pros and cons after a series of interviews with the finalists. Even after that entire process is completed and a candidate is selected, the work is not over. The committee or a subcommittee should be responsible for monitoring the new CEO's progress through the first stages of employment. In all cases, a newly hired CEO should be given an unambiguous, one-year contract that can be renewed for three to five years based on whether the candidate was the right match for the organization.

When Louis Gerstner was named CEO of IBM, he said during his first hundred days, ". . . we're going dark for a bit while we assess the task at hand." He wanted to understand the organization, get to know the staff, figure out the nuts and bolts and discover the strengths and weaknesses of the organization that he was now running. He didn't come in with grand ideas and visions of change before he understood what changes were necessary and what the timing of those changes should be. He didn't spend his time at headquarters. During the first few days and weeks as CEO, he chose to visit the branch offices and attend international managers' meetings. Gerstner said, "The last thing IBM needs right now is vision." What he was saying is that he had to attend first to the business at hand and that business was making sure that he had the right people in the right places, reviewing and understanding the budget, and determining customer and client service needs. This is a good and sound approach for any new CEO. Give yourself time to learn, learn what you do not know, use the people around you to help fill in the blanks, accumulate facts and data on which to base your decisions, and build a team around you of bright, able, creative, and challenging people whom you trust. That's the best way to proceed as you enter the new world of the organization that you're now leading. Bring the board and staff along with you. A good leader must have sound troops who are willing to follow. Don't be too far out ahead or behind them, but rather develop a relationship that allows the entire group to be on the same page and advance in lockstep.

Summary

- The process of succession is one that all organizations will experience at one time or another. Succession of leadership is an essential part of organizational planning and development.
- Boards have the primary responsibility for planning the succession of the CEO. The chief executive also has the primary responsibility for the development of succession plans for all other personnel under his or her jurisdiction.
- Some boards and professionals are resistant to succession planning, fearing that the process will be time consuming and not productive.
- Succession planning involves a careful ongoing process of interviews, reference checking, consideration of personal characteristics, and most importantly, a prospective employee's acceptance and identification with the mission and function of the organization.
- A retiring chief executive needs to be aware of his feelings with respect to the impending process of his leaving the organization. Many CEOs do not effectively address this issue.
- Executives who remain as consultant or special advisor need to be aware of their new role and have clarity with respect to their relationship with their successor and with the board.
- Executives who are retiring might well find collegial mutual-aid groups to share their concerns and feelings about this important life-changing transition.

- Many boards need help from outside sources in the process of selecting a CEO.
- The expectations of the new CEO should be realistic and tailored to the time required to effectively understand the organization and its culture, reputation, and programmatic services.

References

Brooks, David. 2009. "The Great Gradualist," *New York Times* (August 27).

Chan, Sewell. 2009. "Food Stamp Enrollment Surges to 1.6 Million," *New York Times* (October 22).

Cohen, Todd. 2006. "Cultivating Effective Media Relations and Marketing," in *Effectively Managing Nonprofit Organizations*. NASW Press, Washington D.C.

Collins, Jim. 2005. *Good to Great and the Social Sectors*. HarperCollins, New York.

Collins, Jim. 2009. *How the Mighty Fall: Why Some Companies Never Give In*. Harper Collins, New York.

Coltoff, Phillip. 2006. *The Challenge of Change*. The Children's Aid Society, New York.

Crutchfield, Leslie R., and Heather McLeod Grant. 2007. *Forces for Good: The Six Practices of High Impact Nonprofits*. (1st ed.). Chapter 2: "Advocate and Serve"; Chapter 5: "Nurture Not-for-Profit Networks." Jossey-Bass, San Francisco.

Eadie, Douglass C. 2006. "Building the Capacity to Lead Innovation," in *Effectively Managing Nonprofit Organizations*. NASW Press, Washington D.C.

Edwards, Richard L., and John A. Yankey, eds. 2006. *Effectively Managing Nonprofit Organizations*. NASW Press, Washington D.C.

Ellison, Jennifer, Susan Parish, and Janice K. Parish. 2006. "Managing Diversity," in *Effectively Managing Nonprofit Organizations*. NASW Press, Washington D.C.

Faust, Drew G. 2009. "Leadership without a Code," *New York Times* (November 1).

Frisch, Bob. 2009. "Myths that Undermine Decision Making" *BusinessWeek* (October 23).

George, William W. 2009. "7 Lessons for Navigating the Storm," *Harvard Business Review* (October 13).

Goodman, Peter S. 2009. "The Recession's Over, But Not the Layoffs," *New York Times* (November 7).

Gosling, Jonathan, and Henry Mintzberg. 2003. "The Five Minds of a Manager" *Harvard Business Review* (November 1).

Guthrie, Kendall, and Justin Louie. 2007. "Strategies for Assessing Policy Change Efforts: A Prospective Approach" (Vol. XIII, No. 1), *Harvard Family Research Project*.

Heavey, Susan. 2009. "U.S. Deaths Attributed to Lack of Insurance," *Reuters* (September 17).

Herbert, Bob. 2009. "A Recovery for Some," *New York Times* (November 13).

Holland, Thomas P. 2006. "Strengthening Board Performance," in *Effectively Managing Nonprofit Organizations*. NASW Press, Washington D.C.

Huffman, Kevin. 2009. "Education: Bringing Innovation to Scale" (No. 14), *Democracy—A Journal of Ideas*.

Kaminer, Ariel. 2009. "Warm Intentions Meet Cold Reality," *New York Times* (November 22).

Kennedy, Larry. 2004. *Quality Management in the Nonprofit World*. Reliable Man Books.

Kristof, Nicholas D. 2009. "Priority Test: Health Care or Prisons?," *New York Times* (August 19).

Lipman, Joanie. 2009. "The Measure of Woman," *New York Times* (October 24)

Louie, Justin, and Kendall Guthrie. 2007. "Strategies for Assessing Policy Change Efforts: A Prospective Approach" (Vol. XIII, No. 1), *Harvard Family Research Project*.

MacFarquhar, Neil. 2009. "U.N. Chief Says Working Poor Still Suffer," *New York Times* (September 18).

Mallozzi, Vincent M. 2009. "Budd Schulberg: A Writer Infused with a Fighting Spirit," *New York Times* (August 9).

New York Times. 2009. "Home Alone" (editorial, October 20).

New York Times. 2009. Special Section on Retirement (October 15).

Pelton, Emily, and Richard E. Baznik. 2006. "Managing Public Policy and Government Relations," in *Effectively Managing Nonprofit Organizations*. NASW Press, Washington D.C.

Rampell, Catherine. 2009. "August Joblessness Hit 10% in 14 States and D.C.," *New York Times* (September 18).

Reinhart, Carmen M., and Kenneth S. Rogoff. 2009. *This Time Is Different: Eight Centuries of Financial Follies* (1st ed.). Princeton University Press.

Shapiro, Daniel. 2008. Dealing with the Emotional Aspect of Conflict," *Harvard Mental Health News Letter* (No. 4, November).

Strom, Stephanie. 2009. "Does Service Learning Really Help?," *New York Times* (December 29).

Sullivan, Paul. 2009. "Now Even Millionaires Can See the Benefit of Budgeting," *New York Times* (September 9).

Tosone, Carol. 2009. "*Sotto Voce:* Internalized Misogyny and the Politics of Gender in Corporate America," *Psychoanalytic Social Work* (Vol. 16, January).

Weinbach, Robert W. 2007. *The Social Worker as Manager* (5th ed.). Chapter 2: "The Context of Human Services Management"; Chapter 3: "Historical Origins of Current Approaches"; Chapter 6: "Promoting a Productive Work Environment"; Chapter 8: "Organizing"; Chapter 12: "Becoming an Effective Manager." Allyn & Bacon.

Zencey, Eric. 2009. "G.D.P. R.I.P.," *New York Times* (August 9).

Zimmerman, Eilene. 2009. "Expecting a Baby, but Not the Stereotypes," *New York Times* (November 22).

About the Author

Phillip Coltoff, a national leader and innovator in the field of social services and youth development, led the Children's Aid Society, one of the largest and oldest social agencies in the United States, from 1980 to 2005. During this period of leadership, the Society grew its budget from $10 million to $85 million annually and developed trailblazing programs in teen pregnancy prevention, public school reform, and the reintegration of juvenile offenders. These programs have been replicated in more than 13,000 sites, nationally and internationally.

He currently is the Katherine W. and Howard Aibel Visiting Professor and Executive-in-Residence at New York University's Silver School of Social Work. Coltoff is the recipient of numerous leadership awards, including the prestigious

William S. White award from the U.S. Department of Education. Coltoff is the author of three previous books: *Preventing Child Maltreatment: Begin with the Parent*, *The Challenge of Change*, and *The Crusade for Children*.

Professor Coltoff lives in Manhattan with his wife, Lynn Harman.

Index

Accountability, 4, 8–10, 42, 128, 158

Action research, 130

Administration, 12, 17, 18

Advisory boards, 11, 95, 150, 157

Advocacy, 42, 75, 81, 84–92, 108, 128, 130, 149

Alger, Horatio, 59

Audit committee, 9

Audits, 11, 42, 116, 119, 121, 122

Baznik, Richard E., 86

Berg, Joel, 149

Better Business Bureau, 11, 19, 122

Board of directors
   budget cuts, 27, 28, 33
   communication with, 86
   composition of, 44, 46, 114
   effectiveness, 105, 150
   fiduciary duties, 16, 17
   and fundraising, 113, 114, 125
   issues concerning, 7, 8
   liability issues, 9, 11, 18, 107
   meetings, 10, 11, 19
   nominating committee, 8, 11, 18, 104, 107, 150
   and organizational change, 75, 76, 79, 81, 82
   overview, 14, 15, 18, 19
   public policy, 86, 89, 91
   role of, 14–17, 27, 28, 103–107, 110, 122
   Sarbanes-Oxley requirements, 8, 9
   search committee, 164, 165, 170

Board of directors (*continued*)
  self-assessment, 106, 110
  succession planning, 163–166, 169–173
  terminology, 8, 104
  training, 106, 107, 110, 136
  as volunteers, 149, 150, 152
Board of governors. *See* Board of directors
Board of overseers. *See* Board of directors
Board of trustees. *See* Board of directors
Boys and Girls Clubs, 2, 24, 35, 36, 38, 52
Branding, 52–54
Brooks, David, 53
Budgets, 27, 28, 33, 122, 123, 126, 132, 136, 138, 140, 144
Buffett, Warren, 119, 155, 161

Cash flow, 122
Change
  impact on not-for-profits, 1
  leadership, 96, 97, 99, 101
  in mission, 73–82
  policy change, 130, 131
  and public policy initiatives, 89
  and technology, 141
  theory of, 130, 131, 138
CharityNavigator.com, 11, 12, 19, 122
Chief executive officer (CEO). *See also* Executive director (ED)
  accountability, 128. *See also* Accountability
  fiscal management, 120–123, 125, 126

and fundraising, 115–118
and gender issues, 66, 67, 69
hiring of, 104, 110
leadership, 94, 95, 108–110. *See also* Leadership
legal and regulatory compliance, 10
lifestyle issues, 167, 168
media, dealing with, 51, 54
new hires, 170–173
retirement, 164–169, 172
role of, 14, 15, 17, 103, 107–111, 131, 132
succession planning, 163–165, 172. *See also* Succession planning
and volunteers, 148–150
Chief financial officer (CFO), 119–121, 125, 126
Children
  and change in mission, need for, 76, 77
  and development of social services, 57–62
  government grants for services, 24, 28
  services, 1–3, 32, 37–40. *See also* Children's Aid Society (CAS)
Children's Aid Society (CAS), 59, 60, 62, 63, 75, 85
Churches, 41, 57, 59, 63, 69, 74
Citizenship, 43–45
Cluster evaluation, 130
Coalitions, 4, 29, 85, 86, 91, 110, 120. *See also* Partnerships
Collaborations, 120, 159. *See also* Partnerships
Collins, Jim, 47, 48, 80, 108, 169
Color, use of, 52, 53

Communication, 50, 86–89, 94, 98

Community sanction (public support), 47–49, 54. *See also* Visibility

Compensation
committee, 9
consultants, 10
employees, 18, 133, 134
executives, 9, 10, 104

Confidentiality, 13, 14, 43, 106, 133, 140–142, 165

Conflicts of interest, 8, 9, 11, 18, 84, 126, 138

Consultants, 9, 10, 142, 166, 172

Crisis management, 33, 82, 96, 97

Crowd sourcing, 143

Crutchfield, Leslie R., 89

Culture. *See* Organizational culture

Damage control, 79, 80, 82, 85

Deinstitutionalization, 73, 74

Deliverables (outcomes), 49

Development. *See* Fundraising

Director of development, 30, 114–116, 120, 125

Disaster relief, 41, 146, 154, 155

Discrimination, 38, 134–135, 138, 161

Donors
and economic downturn, 21, 22, 32. *See also* Recession, impact of
and fundraising, 26
giving opportunities, 124, 125. *See also* Trusts
online donations, 142, 143

and use of funds, 118–120
wealthy donors, 21, 22, 113, 114, 120, 124, 125

Duncan, Arne, 158

Eadie, Douglass C., 81

Economic downturn. *See* Recession, impact of

Edwards, Richard L., 104

Effectively Managing Nonprofit Organizations (Edwards and Yankey, eds.), 81, 86, 104, 105

Eligibility for services, 38–43, 45

Employees
compensation, 18, 133, 134
diversity, 44, 46
and HR functions. *See* Human Resources (HR)
IT staff, 140–142
and public policy functions, 87
training, 135–137, 140, 143, 144
work schedule flexibility, 17, 18

Endowments
bequests, 114
board responsibilities, 16, 17, 19, 27, 33
and fiscal management, 121
losses, 3, 23, 32
need for, 123–124
older not-for-profits, 114
restricted funds, 16, 17
spending, 124

Evaluation, 49, 127–132, 137, 138

Evidence-based programs, 30

Executive compensation, 9, 10, 104

Executive director (ED), 10, 29, 33, 94, 104, 115, 125. *See also* Chief executive officer (CEO); Leadership

Executive officers, 44, 46. *See also* Chief executive officer (CEO); Executive director (ED)

Exit strategy, 28

Faust, Drew Gilpin, 99

501(c)3 organizations, 8, 10, 84, 85, 88, 91, 110, 118, 119, 133

Forces for Good: The Six Practices of High Impact Not-for-Profits (Crutchfield and Grant), 89

For-profit social services, 25

Foundations
    grants, 22–23, 30–31, 33, 123–124
    international efforts, 155, 161
    partnership with, 116, 117, 125
    requests for proposals (RFPs), 117, 118, 125

Friendly Visitors, 59, 60, 69

Frisch, Bob, 95

Fundraising
    and board of directors, 113, 114, 125
    CEO, role of, 115–118
    director of development, 30, 114–116, 120, 125
    online donations, 142, 143
    overview, 124, 125
    professional fundraisers, 114
    tips for, 26, 27
    volunteers, 147, 152
    and wealthy donors, 120, 124. *See also* Donors

Gardner, John, 52

Gates, Bill, 119, 155, 161

Gender issues and social work, 65–67, 69. *See also* Women

George, William W., 97, 160

Gerstner, Louis, 171

Goldman-Sachs Foundation, 119

Goldsmith, Barton, 98

Good to Great and the Social Sectors (Collins), 47, 48, 169

Goodman, Peter S., 77

Governance
    accountability, 8–12
    board of directors, 8, 14
    organizational culture, 12–14
    overview, 7, 8, 18, 19
    review of, 44
    Sarbanes-Oxley, 8, 9

Government
    contracts with agencies, 123, 126
    grants, 21, 24, 25, 33
    and public policy issues, 83–86, 91, 92
    and social services, 28–30

Grant, Heather McLeod, 89

Grants
    foundations, 22, 23, 30, 31, 33, 123, 124
    government, 21, 24, 25, 33
    proposals, 30, 33

Growth, 78–82

Guthrie, Kendall, 130, 131

Health insurance, 32, 39, 45, 82–84, 89, 90, 135

Homelessness, 3, 25, 37, 58, 60, 74, 75

How the Mighty Fall (Collins), 80, 108, 169
Human Resources (HR), 14, 19, 132–135, 137, 138
Hunger, 2, 149, 155, 159–161

Impact evaluation, 128, 129, 137. *See also* Evaluation
Incarceration, costs of, 39, 40
Intermediate Sanctions, 10
Internal Revenue Service (IRS), 10
International social welfare
    and globalization, 153, 154, 161
    and non-for-profits, 154–156, 161
    universities, role of, 155–161

Kaminer, Ariel, 149
Kennedy, Larry, 118
Khazei, Allen, 157
Ki-moon, Ban, 159
Kopp, Wendy, 157
Kristof, Nicholas D., 39

Leadership
    advocacy, 86, 87
    board of directors, 15
    change, 79, 80, 96, 97, 99, 101
    characteristics of successful leaders, 94, 95, 98–101, 108–110
    crisis management, 96, 97
    education programs, 158
    effectiveness, 93–96, 100
    managers, role of, 64, 99, 100
    myths, 95, 96
    new CEOs, 171, 172

skills, 53
    and succession planning, 164.
        See also Succession planning
    training, 65, 66
    vision, 77, 78, 80, 89, 93, 94, 98, 100, 108
    women, 66, 67, 158
Legal and regulatory compliance, 8–11, 18, 88, 124, 133–135, 138, 142, 144
Lipman, Joanie, 158
Lobbying, 4, 85, 86, 89, 92
Local not-for-profits, 35, 36, 45
Logos, 52, 53
Louie, Justin, 130, 131

Management
    and leadership, 99, 100. *See also* Leadership
    role of in social services, 64–69
    and technology, 143, 144
Means test, 38, 45
Mental health services, 24, 32, 38, 43, 73, 74
Mergers and acquisitions, 15, 16, 19
Mission. *See also* Mission statement
    changes in, 38, 45, 73–82
    and public policy position, 87, 88
    reassessing, 32, 33
    and services, 37
    and tax-exempt status, 118, 119
    visibility, 48
    and vision, 81
Mission statement, 71–73, 81
Multiculturalism, 43–45

National not-for-profits, 35, 45
Nominating committee, 8, 11, 18, 104, 107, 150
Non-governmental organizations (NGOs), 155
Not-for-profit sector, 2–5, 42, 46, 91

Obesity, 40
One-stop services, 43
Opportunities, 28, 29
Organizational culture, 12–16, 19, 132
Outcome funding, 30
Outcomes (deliverables), 31, 49, 54, 79, 100, 103, 116, 118, 125, 129, 137, 148, 152. *See also* Evaluation
Overhead costs, 12, 19, 121, 122

Participatory evaluation, 130
Partnerships, 4, 15, 16, 29, 31, 85, 110, 117, 120, 125, 136, 157, 158
Pelton, Emily D., 86
Picower Foundation, 23
Policy analysis, 128
Poor Laws of 1601, 56, 68
Process evaluation, 128, 129, 137. *See also* Evaluation
Program self-evaluation, 130
Prospective evaluation, 130, 131
Protestant ethic, 55, 56
Prudent investments, 16, 17, 19, 83
Psychology and social work, 63, 69, 74
Public image, 83, 84
Public policy, 83–92

Public relations, 48–52, 79
Public Service Announcements (PSAs), 26

Quality Management in the Nonprofit World (Kennedy), 118

Randolph, A. Phillip, 63
Ratings of not-for-profits, 11, 12, 19
Recession, impact of
  on donors, 21–23
  growing needs for services, 2–4, 32, 39, 159
  on government funding, 3, 24, 123
  unemployment, 3, 39, 77–78
Red Cross, 35, 41, 114
Referrals, 43
Reinhart, Carmen M., 31
Reporting, 11
Request for proposal (RFP), 29, 117, 118, 125
Reserve funds, 3, 17, 27, 114, 123, 124
Restricted gifts, 12, 16, 17, 121, 123
Retirement, 164–169, 172
Revenue sources
  and budgeting, 123. *See also* Budgets
  government, 41, 42, 46, 84, 85, 123, 125
  increasing revenue, 26–29, 32, 33
  location and demographics, effect of, 36, 37
  online donations, 142, 143
  results, need for, 49

and use of funds, 118–120

wealthy donors, 21, 22, 113, 114, 120, 124, 125

Rogoff, Kenneth S., 31

Role of not-for-profits in society, 1, 2

Salvation Army, 62, 74, 114

Sarbanes-Oxley Act (SOX), 8–10, 18

Schulberg, Budd, 53, 54

Schwarts, Eric, 157

Search committee, 164, 165, 170

Section 501(c)3 organizations, 8, 84

Self-dealing, 9

September 11, 2001 attacks, 41, 46

Service learning, 146, 147, 151

Settlement houses, 37, 44, 60, 61, 69, 75

Shapiro, Daniel, 137

Social Darwinism, 56

Social services

   history of, 55–65, 69

   need for, 24, 25

   role of not-for-profits, 31, 32

   system, 42–45

Social welfare, 55. *See also* International social welfare

Social work and social workers

   client privacy policies, 141, 142

   education, 64, 67–69

   history of, 55–65, 69

   international efforts, 155, 156, 161

   managerial roles, 64–69, 140, 141

   role of, 4

The Social Worker as Manager (Weinbach), 64, 141

Software, 142. *See also* Technology

Soros, George, 119

Spheres of service

   described, 35, 36

   and funding, 36, 37

   and multiculturalism, 43–45

   overview, 45, 46

   service base, broadening, 37–43

Staff. *See* Employees

Strategic planning, 28, 105, 106, 131

Strom, Stephanie, 146

Sturz, Herb, 74

Succession planning, 163–166, 169–173

Taglines, 52, 53

Tax-exempt organizations. *See* 501(c)3 organizations

Technology

   client privacy policies, 141, 142

   importance of, 140–143

   IT staff, 140–142

   online donations, 142, 143

   overview, 143, 144

   use of, 31, 139

   and visibility, 49

Theory of Change, 130, 131, 138

This Time Is Different: Eight Centuries of Financial Follies (Reinhart and Rogoff), 31

Tone at the top, 14, 19, 132

Tosone, Carol, 66, 67

Trade associations, 86

Training and education
  board of directors, 106, 107, 110
  employees, 135–137, 140, 143, 144
  volunteers, 148, 152
Transparency, 8, 10, 11, 27, 49, 83, 86–88, 92, 125, 132
Trust, 30, 43, 50, 171
Trusts, 114, 124, 125

"Undeserving poor," 56, 69
Unemployment, 3, 22, 28, 37, 39, 74, 77–78, 90
United Way, 16, 52, 114
Universities
  education for board and staff, 106, 136
  endowments, 16, 17, 114. *See also* Endowments
  foundations, gifts from, 118, 119
  investments, 23
  overseers, 104. *See also* Board of directors
  role of, 5, 155–161

Values, 12–14
Visibility, 26, 48–52, 54. *See also* Community sanction (public support)
Vision, 73–82, 89, 93, 94, 98, 100, 108
Volunteers
  background checks, 148
  board members, 149, 150, 152
  corporate, 147
  fundraising, 147, 152
  growth of voluntarism, 146, 147
  and management, 147–152
  motives, 150, 151
  need for, 145, 151
  recognition, 149, 150
  recruiting, 148, 172
  students, 146, 147, 151
  training, 148, 152

Websites
  and branding, 53
  development office, responsibilities of, 115, 124
  importance of, 49, 143, 144
  minutes of meetings, posting on, 10
  reports, posting on, 11, 121
Weinbach, Robert W., 64, 141
Women
  discrimination, 135, 161
  and health insurance, 89, 90, 135
  inequal treatment of, 161
  international issues, 158, 159
  as managers, 66, 67, 69, 158
  and social work, 65–67, 69
  unemployment, 90
Workplace, 14, 17, 18

Yankey, John A., 104
Yeh, Raymond T., 98
YMCA and YWCA, 24, 38, 41, 44

Zencey, Eric, 32
Zimmerman, Eilene, 135